LINCOLN HALL  AT THE UNIVERSITY OF ILLINOIS

MW00334043

John Hoffmann

LINCOLN HALL

at the University of Illinois

UNIVERSITY OF ILLINOIS PRESS   URBANA & CHICAGO

© 2010 by the Board of Trustees
of the University of Illinois
All rights reserved
Manufactured in China

1 2 3 4 5 C P 5 4 3 2 1

∞ This book is printed on acid-free paper.

Hoffmann, John.
Lincoln Hall at the University of Illinois / John Hoffmann.
p.   cm.
Includes bibliographical references and index.
ISBN 978-0-252-03523-4 (cloth : alk. paper)
ISBN 978-0-252-07708-1 (pbk. : alk. paper)
1. Lincoln, Abraham, 1809-1865—Monuments—Illinois.
2. University of Illinois (Urbana-Champaign campus).
Lincoln Hall. I. Title.
LD2385.l5h6 2009
378.773'66—dc22   2009036214

Library of Congress Cataloging-in-Publication Data

CONTENTS

LINCOLN HALL  AT THE UNIVERSITY OF ILLINOIS

TO EDUCATE AND INSPIRE

FILL EACH OF THE 12 PANELS ON
NORTH & SOUTH ELEVATIONS WITH
LETTERING.

NOTE:
THE 26 OVAL PANELS IN THESE
ENTRANCE AND THE 10 FIGURE
PANELS IN FRONT ARE INCLUDED
IN MODELING ALLOWANCE.

METAL RIDGE.

SLATE ROOF.

PLAN OF CORNICE SOFFIT.

TILE BOLTED TO L

½ SECTION FOR
COPPER CORNICE.

GLASS   GLASS

MODEL #1

MODEL #1

MODEL #2

MODEL #3

MODEL #4

- BRICK -

MODEL #2

MODEL #5

3RD FLOOR LINE.

2ND FL LINE.

*A*N 1909 the State of Illinois appropriated $250,000 for a building at the University of Illinois "dedicated to the study of the humanities."[1] That year being the centennial of Abraham Lincoln's birth, the building was named Lincoln Hall. This book, occasioned by the bicentennial of Lincoln's birth, sketches the history of Lincoln Hall in its early years and gives particular attention to the Lincoln art—the collection of panels, portraits, and inscriptions—that adorns the building.

Those who planned Lincoln Hall anticipated that its decorative features would educate and inspire. A University publication issued when the building was dedicated in 1913 stated, "There is seldom a time when young men and women are not to be seen studying these inscriptions and panels." It continued, "Students and professors at work in this building, or even passing along the walks about it, should be in daily and hourly remembrance of what this man and his co-workers did for the American people." The *Alumni Quarterly* editorialized, in terms characteristic of the Progressive era, that Lincoln Hall would impress upon "the procession of young citizens" who entered it "something not merely of scholarship by departments, but of the wisdom and patriotism of the democracy of learning." As *The Survey*, a reform journal of the day, opined: "Perhaps even the state legislators are 'building better than they knew' in raising a shrine to patriotism to mark the fall of the bribery and exploitation among them which have shamed the state and the very name of Lincoln"—undoubtedly alluding to the recent ouster of an Illinois senator from the U.S. Senate.[2]

Who shaped this optimistic appeal to the spirit of Lincoln? Who proposed, planned, and carried out the artistic program of Lincoln Hall? Who was responsible for the panels depicting Lincoln's life and times on the east (Quad) side of the building, for the excerpts from his writings that are quoted on the flanking north and south facades, for the portraits of his contemporaries that frame those excerpts, and for the names that are emblazoned on the escutcheons at each corner of the building? In short, who was responsible for "this new and distinguished piece of biography . . . issued in a single edition of one volume and one copy"?[3]

Photograph on page 1: An early photograph, ca. 1914, of Lincoln Hall. A legislative appropriation made possible the construction of the building, which accommodated several departments in the humanities.

PLANS FOR LINCOLN HALL

ON JUNE 14, 1909, the General Assembly of the State of Illinois, asked to fund a dozen buildings at the University, authorized one: "Whereas, the University of Illinois has grown with such great rapidity as to outrun all facilities in building and equipment which have been thus far provided," and whereas the Trustees of the University had appealed for $3,250,000 to build or enlarge twelve buildings, the legislature appropriated $250,000 for a single building, a "new university hall."[1]

The Board of Trustees, meeting one month after this appropriation, located the new building south of the Woman's Building (erected in 1905, now much enlarged and known as the English Building) and close to the Auditorium (erected in 1908, now known as Foellinger Auditorium). A few weeks later, W. Carbys Zimmerman, the state architect, had finished the first of several sketch plans for "the new University Hall." Throughout the design process, he planned a building that would eventually form a square, only half of which was funded in 1909. The long side, the main facade, would face east. Extending back

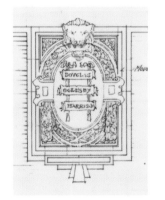

from that facade would be two wings of equal length. Those wings would later be lengthened and would be connected on the west side to complete the square.

Zimmerman regarded this "straightforward, simple grouping of parts" as the best design for the new building.[2]

University president Edmund J. James at first proposed that the building be four stories instead of three, using a design Zimmerman had created for the Physics Building (erected in 1908, now the Materials Science and Engineering Building). For aesthetic as well as financial reasons, however, Zimmerman favored three stories on each facade for the new building. This design would respect the three-story cornice line of the other buildings that were beginning to define the Quad. To satisfy James, however, Zimmerman created a fourth or attic floor, which is lit by full-size dormer windows on the interior or court side of the building but only by window slits on the front. Interestingly, no one involved in planning the building referred to it as exemplifying any particular architectural style, although its symmetrical three-story facade and

This picture of Lincoln Hall under construction was taken from the steps of the Auditorium in January 1911. By that point, both windows and roof had been framed. The window slits on the fourth or attic floor, immediately below the eaves, were still visible. However, the contractor had not yet installed the terra cotta panels in the spandrels between the second and third floors.

Edmund J. James (1855–1925), leader of the University of Illinois from 1904 to 1920, secured funding for Lincoln Hall in 1909, the centennial of Lincoln's birth.

W. Carbys Zimmerman (1859–1932) held the position of State Architect during Governor Charles S. Deneen's administration, 1905–13. In those years, he designed Lincoln Hall, the Physics Building, the Armory (enlarged in 1927), and the Stock Pavilion for the University of Illinois.

its sheltering roof might be described as a Renaissance Revival design with Prairie-esque detailing.[3]

On November 10, 1909, Evarts B. Greene, professor of history and dean of the College of Literature and Arts, recommended to James "that the building be designated as Lincoln Hall." James found the name "rather a good suggestion" and forwarded it to Zimmerman. To Zimmerman, the name was "a most excellent one, particularly as the exterior as now designed in its simplicity, straight-forwardness and dignity, makes this specially appropriate." Zimmerman's general plan for the structure and his recommendation that "the name of Abraham Lincoln Hall be given to this building" were approved by the Trustees on November 26.[4]

During the next two years, Greene provided the data about Lincoln and his times that would define the artistic program for the building in Lincoln's honor. James turned to Greene at every point, being himself mainly concerned to "put this building through on the double quick."[5]

Greene favored plans that would maximize the building's space. The design, he wrote, "should be simple, depending for its effect upon proportion rather than ornament." Wanting "the maximum amount of area possible within the limits of cost," Greene objected to one of Zimmerman's sketches for the building because it would mean "a serious sacrifice of efficiency to ornamental considerations." When Zimmerman proposed to stay within budget by cutting as many as three bays out of the six he originally planned for each wing, Greene

Zimmerman's presentation drawing for Lincoln Hall.
The five bays on each side of the main entrance were built
as shown, but the number of bays on each side was cut from
six to five. Zimmerman completed this drawing after the
Trustees named the building in November 1909.

Zimmerman's drawings include the elevation and a section of a typical bay of the front and sides of Lincoln Hall. He planned for a terra cotta panel between the second and third floors of each bay. He also planned for escutcheons under the eaves of the bays at each corner of the building.

Evarts B. Greene (1870–1947), professor of history, provided the ideas for the "Lincoln" aspect of Lincoln Hall—the name of the building as well as the scenes to depict, the excerpts to inscribe, and the list of Lincoln's contemporaries to portray on the building.

again recommended space over ornamentation. Greene would avoid such a drastic cut "by omitting the decorative design on the exterior terra cotta panels and leaving plain surfaces. . . . this would not essentially affect the general architectural design."[6]

Throughout the design process, Zimmerman conferred with James M. White, professor of architectural engineering, who would serve as the on-site supervising architect. For a time, the two men differed regarding Zimmerman's three-story plan.[7] White also complained that Zimmerman left some of the work to less-skilled architects in his office in Chicago, and that he did not give White enough time to study the plans or to review them with Greene and other heads of the "literary departments" that would occupy the building. But together White and Zimmerman grappled with the mandate to keep the total cost under $200,000—a limit that allowed part of the legislative appropriation to be used for "equipment." Such equipment included not only books for the new departmental libraries to be housed in Lincoln Hall but also "illustrative material" for "enriching instruction" in every literary department. The use of maps and charts in History, casts and photographs in Classics, and lantern slides across the curriculum would make classrooms for the humanities comparable to the laboratories for "physics, chemistry, or electrical engineering," according to Greene. Furthermore, a building so equipped would provide a model "for the high schools in which our graduates are to teach." President James, who also supported reserving funds for equipment, wrote, "Some of

James M. White (1867–1933, class of 1890) taught architecture. In 1907 he became the University's Supervising Architect. In that position, he was either the architect or the consulting architect for nearly eighty buildings, including Lincoln Hall.

our Trustees have never believed that English or German or Economics needs any thing for equipment." The new building was a chance to prove otherwise.[8]

Bidding on the building's construction went through several stages. Twenty-one contractors applied for copies of the plans, eleven submitted bids ranging from $275,536 to $306,000, and seven revised their estimates to accord with changes in the plans. English Brothers of Champaign, a firm still in business, submitted the low bid of $198,000, which the Trustees accepted on April 12, 1910.[9]

To ensure that at least $50,000 would be available for equipment, to maximize interior space and yet retain

historical ornamentation on the exterior, Zimmerman and White had trimmed the projected costs, mainly by using less expensive building materials and by omitting one bay on each wing.[10] In the final plans, the building retained ten bays across the front or east facade (five on each side of the main entrance), but the north and south wings were cut from the plan's original six bays to five.

Lincoln Hall was faced in brick, while the windows were framed with terra cotta, the porcelain finish of which could be easily cleaned. To save money, copper rather than terra cotta was used for the cornice, including the escutcheons at the corners of the building. Similarly, "for reasons of economy," the building's exterior decorative program was carried out in terra cotta rather than in stone. Rather than spend an estimated $3,000 for sculpture, Zimmerman earmarked $1,000 for a contract with the American Terra Cotta and Ceramic Company to make a series of terra cotta panels, portraits, and inscriptions.[11]

This early view of Lincoln Hall shows five bays on the north side. The Class of 1912 contributed the stone column and circular bench near the building. In the foreground is Burrill Avenue, a dirt road before it was paved and long before it became a major campus sidewalk.

PLANNING LINCOLN HALL'S LINCOLN ART

THE BUILDING'S decorative program, like its name, stemmed from Greene's suggestions. On April 15, 1910, Zimmerman, having nearly completed modifications in the plans the contractor would use, wrote to President James for suggestions as to the decorative "tablets, names and dates." James promptly asked Greene to consider "the historic side" of the matter: "What scenes from the life of Lincoln" should be depicted? Who among "governors, or distinguished statesmen, or what not" should be recognized? For advice on the "artistic side," James asked White, the supervising architect, to appoint a committee that would include Greene; N. Clifford Ricker, professor of architecture; Newton Alonzo Wells, professor of architectural decoration; and Edward J. Lake, professor of art and design.[1]

Greene soon outlined his ideas for "pictorial representations on the panels along the east front" of Lincoln Hall. In the same letter, Greene provided his "suggestions regarding inscriptions for the exterior panels" on the wings of the building. In Zimmerman's design, these panels—ten scenes from Lincoln's life and times on the front of the building, and ten excerpts from his writings on the sides—became the spandrels between the second- and third-floor windows.[2]

Zimmerman decided to frame the large rectangular panels on the front and side facades by roundels. At first he planned to put medallion portraits of Lincoln's contemporaries next to the biographical panels on the front facade, but then he placed them next to the Lincoln texts on the sides of the building. This change made it possible to use the roundels on the front for the year of each scene.

Thus, for example, the vignette showing Lincoln as a rail splitter, when he first came to Illinois, would have "18" to the left and "30" to the right of the scene. Tablets at the main entrance would give Lincoln's birth and death dates, "AD 1809" and "AD 1865." This decorative program was completed by escutcheons below the cornice at each corner of the building that would give the names of those portrayed on the sides.

Again, it was Greene who proposed the particular Lincoln contemporaries who should be commemorated in the portraits and on the escutcheons.[3] In short, Greene took the lead in formulating the historical program presented on the facades of Lincoln Hall. An efficient and tactful administrator, so modest as to be remembered for his "instinctive self-effacement," Greene was an ideal lieutenant for James.[4] A bachelor who lived with one or the other of his sisters in a house at the end of Wright Street,[5] Greene had the pleasure of watching the new building's construction from his home.

The Rail Splitter, one of the scenes from Lincoln's life and times, flanked by the year of the scene.

CONSTRUCTION

Opposite: One of the contractor's workers stands at the southeast corner of the structure, while others are visible at the top of the second floor.

$\mathcal{E}$ARLY IN 1910, before English Brothers began building Lincoln Hall, five large elms, planted in 1869, had to be cleared from the site. Could they be transplanted? Although Jens Jensen, the leading landscape architect of the day, was somewhat optimistic about moving the trees successfully, President James evidently did not ask the Trustees to approve Jensen's plan and the trees were cut down. Drainage of the site was also a concern, for the new building, unless properly tiled, would further "obstruct the natural water course" behind it, making worse a problem pointed out by Cyril G. Hopkins, professor of agronomy, the cellar of whose home across Wright Street (now the site of the University YMCA) was flooded "whenever a torrential rain occur[red]."[1]

As spring came on, Professor White, the supervising architect, arranged for the appointment of a clerk of the works, and construction got under way. On August 10, 1910, a crowd gathered to witness the laying of the cornerstone. By that time, English Brothers had laid the stone and brick foundations and soon would frame the first and second floors. At the ceremony, William L. Abbott, president of the Board of Trustees, declared that it was University policy to erect buildings "that would endure."[2]

William L. Abbott (1861–1951), Trustee of the University from 1905 to 1923, was intimately involved in the planning and construction of Lincoln Hall and many other buildings on campus. At the Chicago Edison Company (Commonwealth Edison), he was the Chief Operating Engineer. The university's Abbott Power Plant was named in his honor.

MAKING THE TERRA COTTA

Work on Lincoln Hall proceeded apace against a completion deadline of July 12, 1911. The American Terra Cotta and Ceramic Company, responsible for the building's decoration, shipped in good time the terra cotta for the windowsills and frames on the second and third floors, but it was slow to deliver the ornamental spandrels that divided the windows on those floors. Although delayed in "striking a scheme" to "get this building up" without the spandrels, English Brothers simply bricked up each gap and waited.[1]

For American, one of the leading companies in the production of architectural terra cotta, 1910 was its peak year. Its work, according to a recent study, ranged "in scale from chimney pots to skyscrapers and in complexity from stock cornices for building contractors to elegant bank facades designed by such high-profile architects as Louis H. Sullivan." American's president, William D. Gates, started the company as a tile works, using a bed of clay that he had discovered on his farm near Crystal Lake, Illinois, about forty-five miles northwest of Chicago. He soon was making "terra cotta" (from the Latin for "burnt earth"), a building material that appealed to architects and contractors as more economical and plastic than stone. Gates also led in the development of art pottery known as Teco (a name compounded from the first two letters of "terra" and "cotta"), which became important as the ceramic expression of the Prairie School of architecture.[2]

Although terra cotta readily lent itself to colored surfaces, Zimmerman felt that the terra cotta on Lincoln Hall, including its commemorative features, had to be white, apparently as a clear contrast to the building's red brick facing.

American Terra Cotta's chief modeler during the construction of Lincoln Hall was Kristian E. Schneider, a Norwegian-trained sculptor Louis Sullivan had chosen to model his ornamental work. Schneider is known today for his virtuosity in executing Sullivan's organic and geometrical motifs, but his historical depictions for Lincoln Hall are also distinguished. As Gates wrote in *Common Clay,* the company's publication, Schneider was "the controlling genius and hard-working head" of American's modeling room. "Always pleasant and affable," he was extraordinarily productive. "May his fingertips never wear out."[3]

William D. Gates (1852–1935) briefly practiced
law before going into business making clay
products on land he owned near Crystal Lake,
Illinois, northwest of Chicago. Incorporated as the
American Terra Cotta and Ceramics Company in
1886, his enterprise prospered with the growing
demand for architectural and decorative terra cotta.
Something of his genial personality is captured in
this sketch by Charles Morgan.

Kristian E. Schneider (1864–1935)
modeled Lincoln Hall's Lincoln
art, bringing Greene's ideas to life.

Other Terra Cotta Projects at Illinois

STOCK PAVILION

In designing the Stock Pavilion's facade, W. Carbys Zimmerman drew on early modern Italian precedents. He accentuated the regularity and length of the colonnaded arches, balustrade, and entablature by enlisting Kristian Schneider to model ten animal heads. By duplicating each head four or five times, the company made forty-five roundels for the north facade, facing toward the Auditorium. Schneider populated this frieze with reasonable approximations of a Cotswold sheep and a Shropshire sheep, a Poland china pig and a Yorkshire pig, an Angus bull and a shorthorn bull, a Jersey cow and a Holstein cow, and, finally, a "light horse" and a "heavy horse." He placed two more Cotswold rams on the east end of the Pavilion and two more Yorkshire pigs on the west. This plethora of animals illustrated what had been described as Schneider's "unbelievable virtuosity."[1]

The original facade was demolished in 1958, and Schneider's animal roundels were lost—all except two, which now occupy the office of a professor of animal sciences.[2]

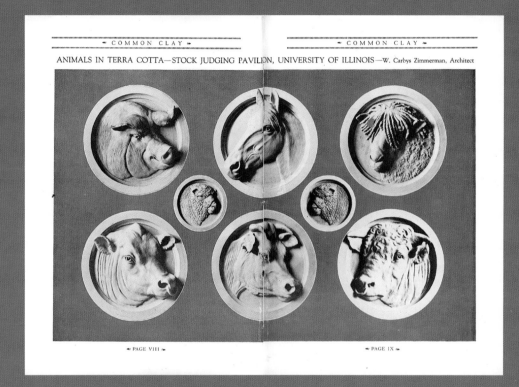

▸ COMMON CLAY ◂   ▸ COMMON CLAY ◂

ANIMALS IN TERRA COTTA—STOCK JUDGING PAVILION, UNIVERSITY OF ILLINOIS—W. Carbys Zimmerman, Architect

◂ PAGE VIII ▸   ◂ PAGE IX ▸

Soon after Kristian Schneider made Lincoln Hall's terra cotta panels, he modeled ten animal heads that were repeated on a frieze extending across the north facade of the Stock Pavilion. Only two of the heads, a Yorkshire pig and a Cotswold sheep, survive.

CERAMICS BUILDING

In 1905, William D. Gates, American Terra Cotta's president and a leader in the Illinois Clay Manufacturers' Association, was among the most active lobbyists in securing legislative support for a Department of Ceramics, renamed the Department of Ceramics Engineering in 1915. Completed in 1916, the Ceramics Building was not only a showpiece for the ceramics industry but also the American Terra Cotta and Ceramics Company's most colorful contribution to the campus. James B. Dibelka, who succeeded Zimmerman as state architect, incorporated richly varied terra cotta into interior columns and into the doorways, mullions, capitals, and escutcheons on the exterior. According to a connoisseur of art pottery, the "compounded and abstracted vegetal forms" of these features, which seemed to "blend elements of corn, bamboo, and flowers," resembled the work of Fritz Albert and Fernand Moreau, designers of American Terra Cotta's Teco pottery.[3]

The Ceramics Building, unlike Lincoln Hall, gave the American Terra Cotta Company a chance to display colored tile. The greens and blues adapted two colors in the palette used in the company's famous Teco pottery.

The Vivarium

It was evidently Gates himself who executed the most imaginative example of American Terra Cotta's work on campus, the plaques on the Vivarium. The Vivarium and its detached wings served initially as laboratories for Entomology and Zoology. They are now known as the Victor E. Shelford Vivarium, in honor of a pioneer ecologist, and are used by the Department of Animal Biology and the Program in Ecology, Evolution, and Conservation Biology.

Two bas relief ceramic plaques composed of matte green Teco tiles enliven the sides of the Vivarium. They depict aquatic life in a composition that is more imaginative than realistic. That Gates placed a marine scene on a land-locked campus, and that he decorated a serious scientific center with such a playful tableau, might seem to illustrate his sense of humor. In fact, the Vivarium's panels closely resemble a terra cotta plaque, made before 1908, that visitors first saw when they approached American Terra Cotta's office and display room. Gates displayed a similar plaque at the Clay Products Exposition in Chicago in 1912, and it is apparent that he had the piece remodeled again for the Vivarium. The pair of terra cotta plaques on the Vivarium gave the campus a unique example of Art Nouveau design.[4]

Gates concluded his contribution to campus architecture by installing a terra cotta panel on each side of the Vivarium, including this one on the east facade.

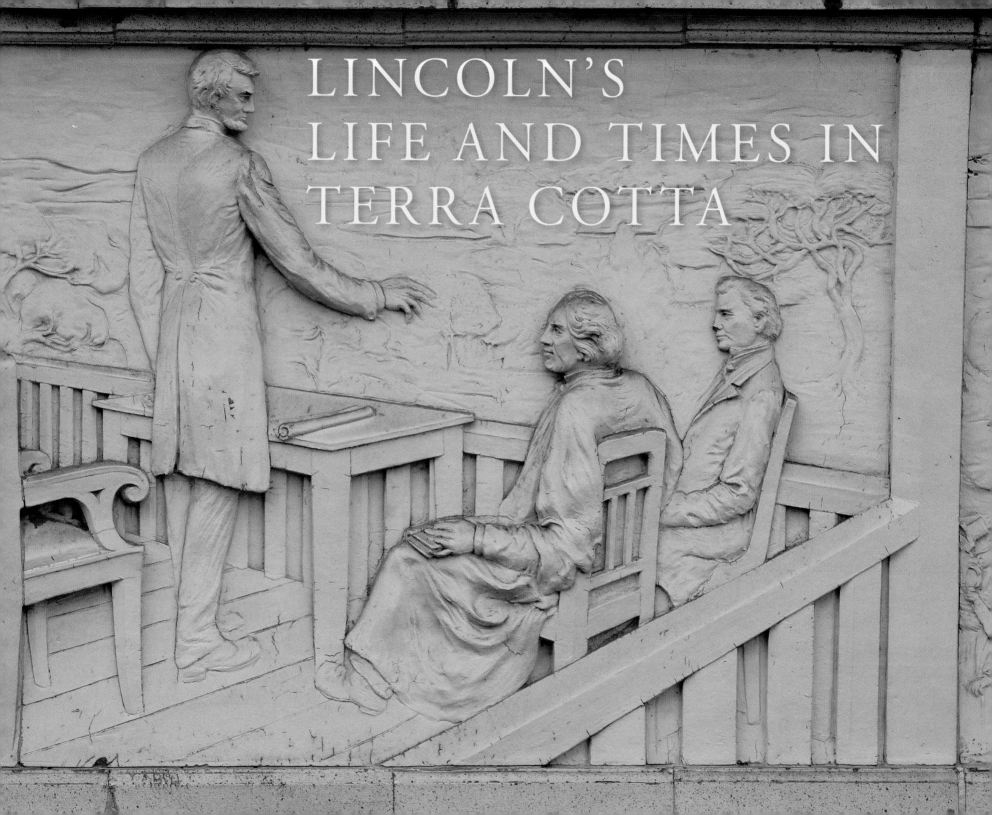

LINCOLN'S
LIFE AND TIMES IN
TERRA COTTA

Kristian Schneider designed the biographical panels on the front (east side) of the building and the portraits of Lincoln's contemporaries on the north and south facades. Pictures of the panels were first published in 1912 in *The Clay-Worker,* an industry publication. William Gates probably wrote "A New Life of Lincoln," the text that went with the pictures. Schneider "required the best part of a year's study" to prepare the panels, according to the article. To depict "the Statesman of the Sangamon," he was said to have culled details from Lincoln biographies, visited historical spots, and collected anecdotes from the families of those who remembered Lincoln. Perhaps such sources stimulated Schneider's imagination in visualizing Lincoln's life, but for the people in those scenes and the portraits of Lincoln's contemporaries, he was probably indebted to Herbert Wells Fay, the editor of the *DeKalb Review* and later custodian of the Lincoln Tomb. Fay had built a huge collection of photographs of historical figures, including Lincoln, and conducted a "portrait loan agency" for hundreds of publications.

"I wish on my own behalf and that of the University," Zimmerman wrote to Fay, "to express my appreciation of what you have done for us."[1]

Schneider was kept busy with many projects. "We have had our moulding room in such a violent rush lately," as Gates explained on August 14, 1911, that Schneider had no time for Lincoln Hall. If President James was determined to dedicate the building on October 27 or 28, Zimmerman could only suggest that "some plaster panels [be] put in place temporarily." Delays in finishing the panels, along with other construction delays—and also the suitability of dedicating the building on Lincoln's birthday—postponed the dedication until February 12, 1913. Most of the classrooms, offices, and departmental libraries were first used in the 1911–12 academic year, prior to the dedication.[2]

The artistic work that went into the panels Schneider finally completed was his own ("K. Schneider" is inscribed in the corner of each panel), but Evarts Greene, writing to Zimmerman on May 25, 1910, had suggested the subject of every scene.

American Terra Cotta
Company's master modeler
inconspicuously signed
"K. Schneider" in the lower
right corner of each of
Lincoln Hall's biographical
panels.

The length of the spandrels required that the panels
be long and thin (nearly 9½' wide by 2½' high), but
at these dimensions the panels were often too wide for
Schneider's scenes. He was obliged at times to fill the
space on either side of the central group with woods and
rivers, platform occupants and distant crowds, and ranks
of soldiers and military paraphernalia. In addition, the
constricted height of the panels did not easily accommodate standing figures, especially Lincoln's.

There is no uniform title for each of the ten panels.
They are referred to in different ways in the articles about
them in *The Clay-Worker* and *Common Clay*.[3]

I. *The Rail Splitter* (1830)

Greene proposed "A scene typical of Lincoln's life as
frontiersman, bringing out the log-cabin and rail
splitter *motif*." Schneider duly pictured Lincoln at
work, piles of split rails near him. A log cabin and the
Sangamon River appear faintly on the left side of the
panel. (Schneider also depicted the stumps of trees, as if
they had been cut down by a saw, not felled by Lincoln's
axe.) "The atmosphere is strikingly Lincolnesque,"
Gates wrote. "The spirit of the land—the field, the for-
est and the stream—from which Lincoln sprang and
which gave to him that elemental strength to do and
to endure, pervades the scene." (The full panel appears
on p. 12.)

2. *The Boatman* (1831)

Greene proposed "Some representation of Lincoln's life on the Mississippi" and suggested that "the slavery idea might be introduced here," since Lincoln as a young man had witnessed aspects of slavery when he had flatboated to New Orleans. But Greene hesitated over Schneider's depiction of Lincoln, sitting on his loaded batteau, watching a slave auction on the Mississippi—an experience that, as Gates put it, caused Lincoln "to vow that he would use his strength to drive the curse of slavery from the land." Greene doubted that Lincoln had ever seen a slave sale that so affected him. It was a "story of rather doubtful authenticity, rejected by some of the best writers on Lincoln." Gates replied: "It is a matter of interpretation whether the figures are intended as physical realities, or the children of Lincoln's thoughts." Schneider reflected this ambiguity by casting the slave auction in such shallow relief that Lincoln seemed to imagine rather than actually see it. Greene then wrote: "I am prepared to withdraw my objection to the second panel referring to the visit to New Orleans."[4]

3. *The Circuit Rider* (1849)

Greene suggested that Schneider depict Lincoln as a circuit rider and referred him to *Life on the Circuit with Lincoln* (1892) by Henry Clay Whitney, an Urbana lawyer. In Schneider's panel, Lincoln approaches a "quaint" courthouse, with Judge David Davis in the background and another lawyer tying his horse to a tree. "According to anecdotal history" reported by Gates, Lincoln is "listening with grace and respectful attention to the plea of an aged widow who has been defrauded by an unscrupulous lawyer." The woman, who had been married to a Revolutionary War soldier, had received a $400 pension from the government, "but her lawyer kept half of it." Lincoln took the case against him "and won it."

Assiduous researchers have revised this "anecdotal history" of the case of *Thomas v. Wright* (1846). Erastus Wright was a prominent citizen of Springfield, School Commissioner of Sangamon County, and a pension agent—but not a lawyer. In 1794, Rebecca Thomas had married a Revolutionary War veteran. They lived in Kentucky before coming to Sangamon County in 1830, but she later returned to Kentucky for two years. Evidently, she felt entitled to payments for that period, but she was mistaken, in Wright's understanding of the complex pension laws. Lincoln, who represented her, first took the case before the Sangamon County Justice of the Peace because the total sum at issue was less than $100. On appeal to the county circuit court, Lincoln, as William H. Herndon recalled forty-odd years later, made an unusually dramatic argument, stressing the privations of Rebecca Thomas's late husband at Valley Forge. Lincoln also castigated Wright—if indeed he followed his cue card to "*Skin Def't.*" The jury found for the widow and awarded $35 in damages. The evidence, especially as embellished by Herndon, was tailor-made for Gates's story of Lincoln the lawyer.[5]

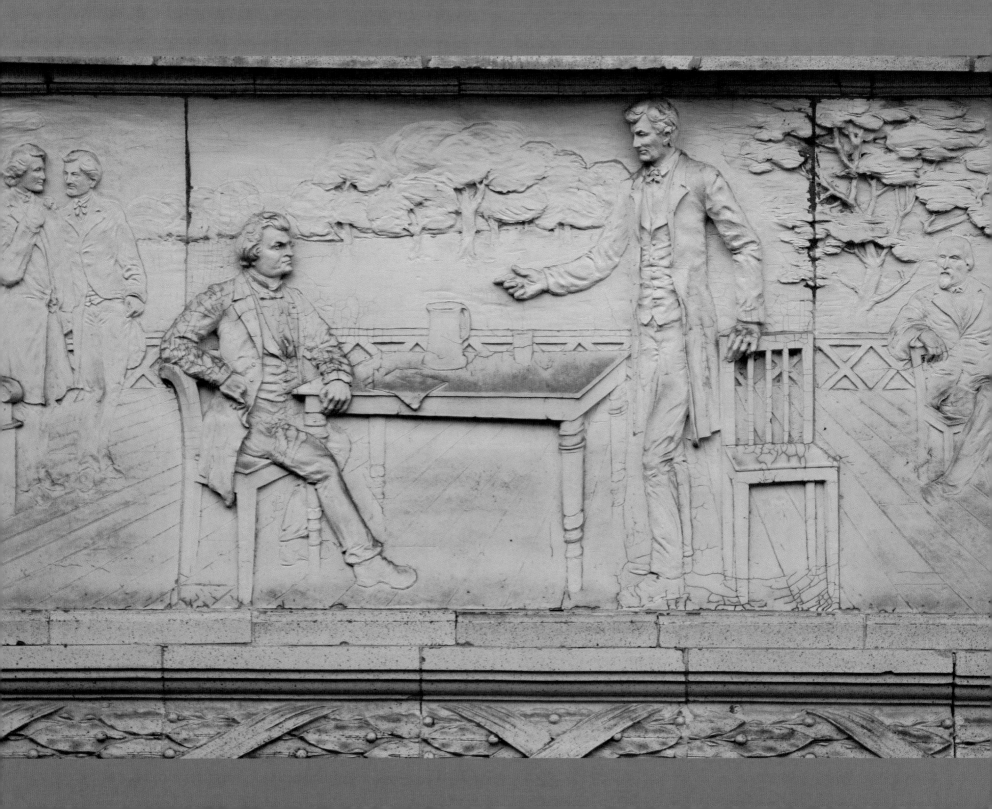

4. *The Debate* (1858)

Greene thought that Schneider could find "pictorial" ideas in the many contemporary descriptions that were included in the Illinois Historical Collections' edition of the Lincoln-Douglas debates, but the benches on the platform and the building in the background make it seem that Schneider developed the scene on his own. Greene suggested that Schneider depict the debate at Galesburg, but Gates placed it at Freeport. Having perhaps heard of Lincoln's "Freeport question," Gates paraphrased what Lincoln had asked earlier in the summer: "Can a house divided against itself long stand? Is it possible for a nation to endure, one-half slave and one-half free?"[6]

5. *The Inauguration* (1861)

Citing the description of the inaugural in John G. Nicolay and John Hay's *Abraham Lincoln: A History* (1890), Greene suggested that Schneider include Chief Justice Roger B. Taney (in judicial robes) and Senator Stephen A. Douglas (holding the President's hat) in the scene. Next to them, toward the railing, Schneider showed President Buchanan, whose term had just ended, and Edward D. Baker, who introduced Lincoln. On the other side of Douglas he placed Mary Lincoln and her cousin, Elizabeth Todd Grimsley (identified by Gates as her niece). "The other figures in this group," Gates explained, "are not worked out with an eye to historic accuracy."

6. *The Call for Volunteers* (1861)

Greene suggested "some symbolical representation of the call for volunteers in April 1861, and the response." Schneider imagined the arrival of the volunteers of a Massachusetts regiment, "the first" to come to the defense of Washington, D.C., and depicted someone other than Lincoln pointing them to the Capitol.

The fall of Fort Sumter had prompted Lincoln to call on the states for seventy-five thousand militia. Gates titled Schneider's panel "We Are Coming, Father Abraham, One Hundred Thousand Strong," an echo of a recruiting song after a later call for troops on July 1, 1862: "We Are Coming, Father Abraham, Three Hundred Thousand More."

7. *The Emancipator* (1863)

For the Emancipation Proclamation, Greene again suggested "some symbolical representation." Schneider provided "Abraham Lincoln, the Savior of the Slave." In Gates's description of the panel, Lincoln, standing near the Potomac, "points to the rising sun of hope and freedom" for the black family bound with chains, the mother and child lying on the ground, and the man "gazing with rapt attention" at the President.

8. *The Gettysburg Speech* (1863)

For "the delivery of the Gettysburg address," which Greene suggested, Schneider again placed Lincoln on a stage, set off by a railing and with seating for nearby auditors. "To his right," according to Gates, sat "a man named Burke," probably Captain Denis F. Burke, who supposedly "had lived in Gettysburg" and who had joined the Union forces "without the formality of enlisting."

Hearing that he had been wounded in action, Lincoln insisted that he occupy "the place of honor upon the platform." Behind him stood Edward Everett, the orator of the day. Burke's story, like the "anecdotal history" of the Revolutionary War widow, pointed to Lincoln's magnanimous spirit, a central theme of Schneider's commemorative panels.

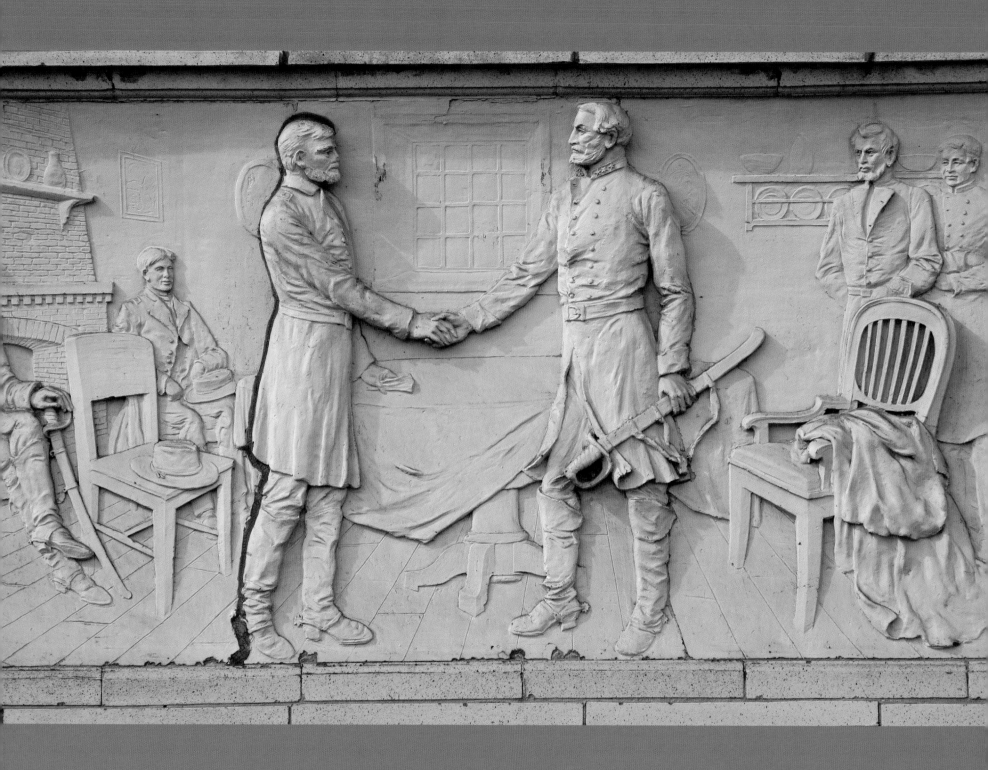

9. *Surrender at Appomattox* (1865)

Greene listed the surrender of Lee to Grant as a subject for pictorial representation. The figure of Lincoln is absent, but Grant appears as his "personal agent in bringing to a close the terrible war." As Gates described it, "Every line in Grant's figure spells force dominant; every line in Lee's bespeaks the poignant bitterness of defeat and the pride of spirit that will not bow the head even to a victor."

10. *The Soldier's Return* (1865)

Greene advanced two ideas for the tenth and last "symbolical representation" on Lincoln Hall. Schneider decided not to depict "the final review of the armies" in the grand march down Pennsylvania Avenue on May 23–24, 1865. Instead he chose to portray "the return of the soldier to peace and civil life" and depicted the theme in a sentimental way: "The aged mother clasps her son once more in her arms," Gates wrote. "The oxen halt in the furrow, as the old father with one hand on the plow turns for his share in the welcome greeting. Gazing at the group from a little distance stands a young woman, a sister or a sweetheart. The mighty Lincoln is departed," Gates concluded, "but peace broods over the rolling prairies."

KSchneider

THE RAILSPLITTER   LINCOLN SERIES NO 1

IF I EVER GET A CHANCE TO HIT
THAT INSTITUTION I'LL HIT IT HARD

THE BOATMAN   LINCOLN SERIES NO 2

A Smaller Set of Panels

In 1920, the American Terra Cotta Company, seeking another market for its Lincoln Hall panels, introduced a "new and smaller" set. Each of these panels was about 3' by 1', approximately one-third the size of the originals set on Lincoln Hall. The new set of panels, according to the *Terra Cotta Factory News,* was "colored in different shadings."[1]

Kristian Schneider numbered each panel, initialed most of them, and gave each the title that is used in the list of panels on Lincoln Hall. For example, he wrote "The Debate" and "Lincoln Series No 4" along the bottom edge of the fourth panel. In that panel, Schneider squeezed into the upper right corner Lincoln's declaration in the House Divided speech:

THE CIRCUIT RIDER   LINCOLN SERIES NO 3

I HOLD THAT THE UNION CANNOT PERMANENTLY EXIST HALF SLAVE AND HALF FREE

THE DEBATE   LINCOLN SERIES NO 4

"I hold that the Union cannot permanently exist half slave and half free." Similarly, he added to the second panel, in which Lincoln appears to be witnessing a slave auction, some words attributed to him regarding slavery: "If I ever get a chance to hit that institution I'll hit it hard."[2] None of the other panels includes a quotation.

Schneider made slight changes in each of the ten panels, not just in the two in which he loosely quoted Lincoln. Thus, in No. 4, he cleared away the trees behind Lincoln and Douglas and left only a pitcher and a cup on the table. He also modified the appearance and the poses of people in every panel.

THE INAUGURATION · LINCOLN SERIES NO 5

THE CALL FOR VOLUNTEERS · LINCOLN SERIES NO 6

The new set found limited success. Unfortunately, also, those panels were only a single inch thick, with the apparent result that most of the small panels, which once ornamented school hallways and other public buildings, became cracked over the years and were discarded.

Today, a full, somewhat battered, light brown set of the panels survives in Decatur, Illinois, having migrated from the county's third courthouse to the city's public library to the Macon County Historical Society. A partial set of eight panels (pictured here), refinished in deep brown, is displayed in the John L. Husmann Elementary School in Crystal Lake, Illinois, having been rescued from storage by Husmann himself.

THE EMANCIPATION   LINCOLN SERIES NO 7

THE GETTYSBURG SPEECH   LINCOLN SERIES NO 8

PRAISE AND CRITICISM

$\mathcal{G}$ATES CELEBRATED "the Lincolnial Pictorial History" that Schneider had created, not only because it encapsulated the life of a great and good man, but also because it exemplified the enduring quality of terra cotta. "Some day, in the far future," he wrote, "these tablets erected in the University of Illinois will be found by some savant and the history of the mythical god Lincoln will be rewritten. Books go the way of men and disappear, but burnt clay has an even chance of immortality."[1]

Less expansively, Evarts Greene referred to the pictorial panels as "ideal representations of the various stages of Lincoln's career."[2] They would be "symbolical" rather than realistic. Written histories lacked details the artist needed, and most photographs of Lincoln's times depicted individuals, not scenes. Schneider's panels conveyed popular ideas about the events they portrayed; and particular scenes, such as Lincoln the Emancipator, were shaped by his generation's views of the past.

Although skilled in modeling architectural ornament (as Louis Sullivan knew), Schneider was inexperienced in representing people. And yet, if the panels are sympathetically assessed, it might be said that Schneider blended the representational and symbolic requirements of the project into an effective ensemble.

The biographical panels on Lincoln Hall were mainly criticized for architectural rather than artistic reasons. As soon as the first panel was delivered, James, Greene, and White met and deemed it "not successful." It was the "lack of relief" or flatness of the terra cotta modeling that troubled them. On March 20, 1911, the company was told to stop work on the project until the first panel could be set in place on the building and judged from there. According to White, James was concerned that the University would be "severely criticised" for spending "money on decoration which has to be viewed with an opera glass [!]. If these panels should prove a failure, it certainly would be a serious setback to our chances for getting any decorative work in future buildings."[3]

On April 1, soon after the first panel had been anchored to the building, several members of the art and architecture faculty "assembled informally" on the site and reached the same conclusion. Such white terra cotta, placed about 30 feet above the ground, was simply too difficult to see clearly. As White reported to James, "There was a unanimous feeling that the type of panel proposed was entirely out of place in such a position on the building; and on the question as to whether the present panel is at all worth while as now set, six voted 'No' and one was in doubt." Moreover, "On the question as to whether the architectural effect of the building would be better if these spandrels were in brick to match the wall of the building, instead of in white, five voted in favor of brick, one in favor of the white, and one was in doubt." The panel itself was not criticized. The group unanimously agreed that "it was impossible to make the panels historical." At best, they could be "but ideal representations" of Lincoln's life.[4]

Professor Charles Melville Moss of the Greek Department also criticized the placement of the first panel. Viewed from immediately in front of Lincoln Hall, "the outlines" on the slab were "fairly distinct," but from a distance they lost their value, and "the dust and smoke of a few years" were likely to "make the lines still more indistinct." Moss also predicted that the placement of the panels would adversely affect the building's proportions. Such light-colored panels between the second and third floors would cause the floors to "merge into an indefiniteness" that would would tend to make the building top heavy and "to depress its height."[5]

The opinion on campus, as James wrote to Zimmerman, was that the first panel was so elevated on the facade as to lack "any architectural or art value." This view was cloaked for a time by the proposal that the State Art Commission be asked for its advice. This step would halt the installation of the panels and give Zimmerman, who had included the panels in the building plans and made the contract with American Terra Cotta, time to express his views of the matter.[6]

As soon as American Terra Cotta learned of the thinking in Urbana, conveyed by tactful letters by White and Greene, Gates exploded. He wrote sarcastically to James: "You have a mighty fine faculty socially and educationally but they are too much for me as critics. Your Mr. White ordered work stopped some little time since. Now Mr. Green [sic] suggests submission to State Art Commission. . . . Unfortunately Michael Angelo, who might have been able to do this work, is not now accessible." Indeed, had Michelangelo been "compelled to submit to the Art Commission before placing his work, Italy might not today have some of her art treasures."[7]

Because American Terra Cotta's expenses already "far exceeded" the amount specified in the contract, Gates felt that he was making a donation to the University. Thus, the critics were "looking a Gift Horse in the Mouth." The company had "done the work" Zimmerman wanted, and the faculty would "have to live with it."[8]

And so they did. On April 22, 1911, the Committee on Buildings and Grounds of the Board of Trustees decided to proceed with the panels in accordance with the contract. Evidently, Zimmerman had sent word that it was too late to change the placement of the panels. It was time for James to set aside the faculty's position and his own doubts. Writing a conciliatory letter to Gates, James expressed regret that Gates had "misunderstood the attitude of [his] colleagues" and thanked Gates for work he "contributed to a considerable degree out of [his] own pocket."[9]

Only one panel, the second of the ten, had been installed in April 1911, and it depicted Lincoln watching a slave auction—a disputed point of history. Mindful of such issues, the Committee on Buildings and Grounds asked Gates to "confer with Dean Greene and the supervising architect with regard to the subjects of the panels." The committee also discussed the whiteness of the panel. Gates lightly touched on these matters when he answered James: "Thanks for yours of 26th. I think the sky has cleared. Have arranged for Deans White and Green [*sic*] to go out [to the terra cotta factory] and inspect and confer, thus introducing color, at least in the inspectors." Despite concerns, the panels being created for Lincoln Hall remained white.[10] The related set of Lincoln panels later marketed by the company used "various shadings" with "satisfactory results," perhaps in response to critics who faulted the bland whiteness of the Lincoln Hall panels.

Letter from William D. Gates, president of the terra cotta company, to University president Edmund J. James, April 19, 1911.

HENRY B. PROSSER
VICE PRESIDENT
JOHN G. CROWE
2ᴺᴰ VICE PRESIDENT

WILLIAM D. GATES
PRESIDENT & GEN'L MANAGER

NEIL H. GATES
SECRETARY
MAJOR E. GATES
TREASURER

THE AMERICAN TERRA COTTA AND CERAMIC COMPANY

Offices 602 Chamber of Commerce Building, Chicago

LONG DISTANCE BELL TELEPHONE
FRANKLIN 1494

Factory-Terra Cotta, Illinois

AUTOMATIC TELEPHONE
No. 3250

April   Chicago April 19ᵗʰ 1911.

President James,
  Illinois University,
  Urbano, Ills.

Mr dear President,

        You have a mighty fine faculty socially and educationally but they are too much for me as critics. Your Mr. White ordered work stopped some little time since. Now Mr. Green suggests submission to State Art Commission and criticises second panel as to whether Lincoln saw any slave sale.

        Now my hands are up. Our contract was to furnish "Modeling for panels to the extent of aproximately One Thousand Dollars". We have already far exceeded that amount and have only four of the ten panels for the front modeled and only part of the heads for the end panels—which your Professor's wish very accurate also.   Unfortunately Michael Angelo, who might have been able to do this work is not now accessible and indeed it just occurs that its just possible that if he had been compelled to submit to the Art Commission before placing his work, Italy might not today have someof her art treasurers.

        Now, as a matter of fact, we have been trying to make a donation and hence your critics have looked to us a little like "looking a Gift Horse in the Mouth". Am satisfied its no use and we will treasure our panels ourselves for we certainly cannot do any better *than we have*.

        Mr. English will not pay us any more until we get finished and "We need the money". This is the work your Architect wanted, but your Professors will have to iive with it.

                Yours truly,
                Wm. D. Gates

LINCOLN QUOTATIONS

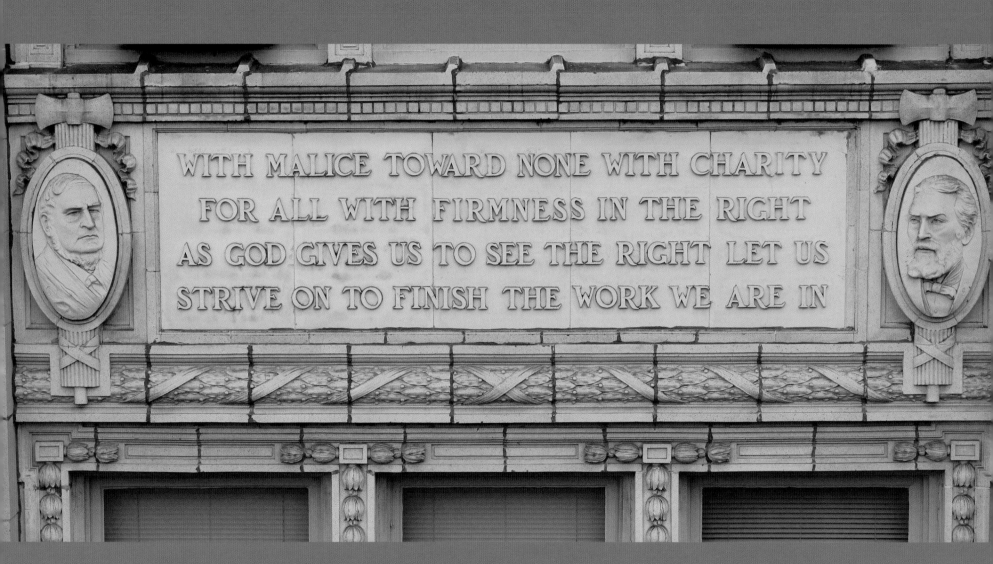

WITH MALICE TOWARD NONE WITH CHARITY FOR ALL WITH FIRMNESS IN THE RIGHT AS GOD GIVES US TO SEE THE RIGHT LET US STRIVE ON TO FINISH THE WORK WE ARE IN

LINCOLN HALL memorialized Lincoln's words as well as scenes from his life and times. Twenty excerpts from Lincoln's writings now appear on the terra cotta panels on the north and south sides of the building. Like the biographical scenes on the front (east) facade, these panels serve as spandrels between the second and third floors.

Evarts B. Greene selected the first ten texts, five on each side of the original structure. In 1928, when the building was expanded, President David Kinley, James's successor, asked Professor Theodore C. Pease and "[his] people" in the Department of History to suggest another ten texts for the new spandrels. The source both Greene and Pease used was the 1905 edition of the *Complete Works of Abraham Lincoln,* which John G. Nicolay and John Hay, Lincoln's secretaries, had first compiled in 1894.

To fulfill his assignment, Pease, perhaps with some assistance from the staff of the Illinois Historical Survey, extracted some thirty passages from Lincoln's writings. From these passages, Pease submitted fifteen quotations.

THAT THIS NATION UNDER GOD
SHALL HAVE A NEW BIRTH OF FREEDOM
AND THAT GOVERNMENT OF THE PEOPLE
BY THE PEOPLE FOR THE PEOPLE
SHALL NOT PERISH FROM THE EARTH

He assumed that "the ten best quotations" had been "selected for the original building," so he could "do no more than take the ten next best." "Undoubtedly," Kinley replied, "some of them will be used." In fact, only six of Pease's selections appear on Lincoln Hall. Kinley himself evidently completed the final list. On the whole, the ten new quotations are indeed less widely known than Greene's ten.[1]

Typographically, all twenty inscriptions regularize a few words and simplify the textual style Lincoln used. Lincoln often italicized a word to emphasize it, and he used more commas than is now standard. The inscriptions ignore italics, capitalize each letter of every word, and omit all periods, commas, and quotation marks. Because of inaccuracies, three panels had to be recast.[2] In the following list, Lincoln's words are capitalized and punctuated according to modern usage.

Each quotation is annotated to indicate its source. Today's standard edition of Lincoln's writings, *The Collected Works of Abraham Lincoln,* is used for this purpose.[3] This work is cited as *CW,* followed by the volume and page number.

The quotations are numbered in the following list so that the panels themselves may be read from left to right, as in a book. The numbering runs across the south facade, from the west end to the east end, and then across the north facade, from the east end to the west end. Thus, numbers 6–15 give the texts Greene selected in chronological order for the original building, while numbers 1–5 and 16–20 give the texts, in no particular order, on the addition.

Portraits of Lincoln's contemporaries appear in the roundels that flank each of the texts Greene chose. Although there is no relation between the portraits and Lincoln's words, the people depicted in each pair of portraits are named after each quotation. (These contemporaries are identified on pages 62–65.)

1. "Let none falter who thinks he is right." Speech on the Sub-Treasury, Springfield, Dec. 26, 1839 (*CW* 1:179).

2. "Let every man remember that to violate the law is to trample on the blood of his father, and to tear the charter of his own and his children's liberty." Speech to Young Men's Lyceum, Springfield, Jan. 27, 1838 (*CW* 1:112).

3. "Free labor insists on universal education." Address before the State Agricultural Society, Milwaukee, Sept. 30, 1859 (*CW* 3:480).

4. "No man is good enough to govern another man without that other's consent." Speech at Peoria, Oct. 16, 1854 (*CW* 2:266).

5. "I believe the declaration that 'all men are created equal' is the great fundamental principle upon which our free institutions rest." Letter to James N. Brown, Oct. 18, 1858 (*CW* 3:327).[4]

6. "Slavery is founded in the selfishness of man's nature. Opposition to it in his love of justice." Speech at Peoria, Oct. 16, 1854 (*CW* 2:271). Horace Greeley (left) and Jonathan Baldwin Turner (right).

7. "'A house divided against itself cannot stand.' I believe this government cannot endure permanently half slave and half free." Speech at Springfield, June 16, 1858 (*CW* 2:461). Charles Francis Adams (left) and Charles Sumner (right).

A HOUSE DIVIDED AGAINST ITSELF
CANNOT STAND
I BELIEVE THIS GOVERNMENT CANNOT ENDURE
PERMANENTLY HALF SLAVE AND HALF FREE

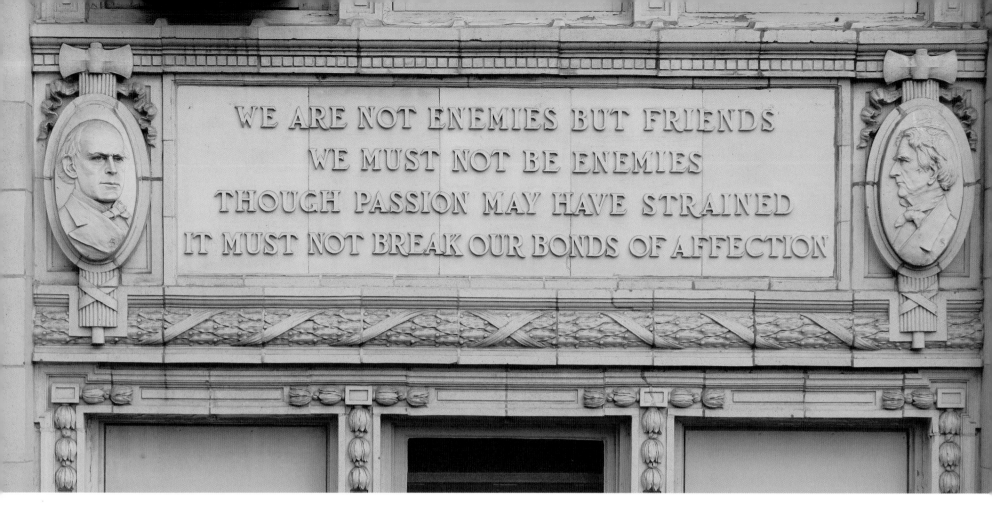

WE ARE NOT ENEMIES BUT FRIENDS
WE MUST NOT BE ENEMIES
THOUGH PASSION MAY HAVE STRAINED
IT MUST NOT BREAK OUR BONDS OF AFFECTION

8. "Let us have faith that right makes might, and in that faith let us to the end dare to do our duty as we understand it." Cooper Institute speech, Feb. 27, 1860 (*CW* 3:550). David G. Farragut (left) and Ulysses S. Grant (right).

9. "I hold that, in contemplation of universal law and of the Constitution, the Union of these States is perpetual." First Inaugural Address, Mar. 4, 1861 (*CW* 4:264). Gideon Welles (left) and Edwin M. Stanton (right).

10. "We are not enemies, but friends. We must not be enemies. Though passion may have strained, it must not break our bonds of affection." First Inaugural Address, Mar. 4, 1861 (*CW* 4:271). Salmon P. Chase (left) and William H. Seward (right).

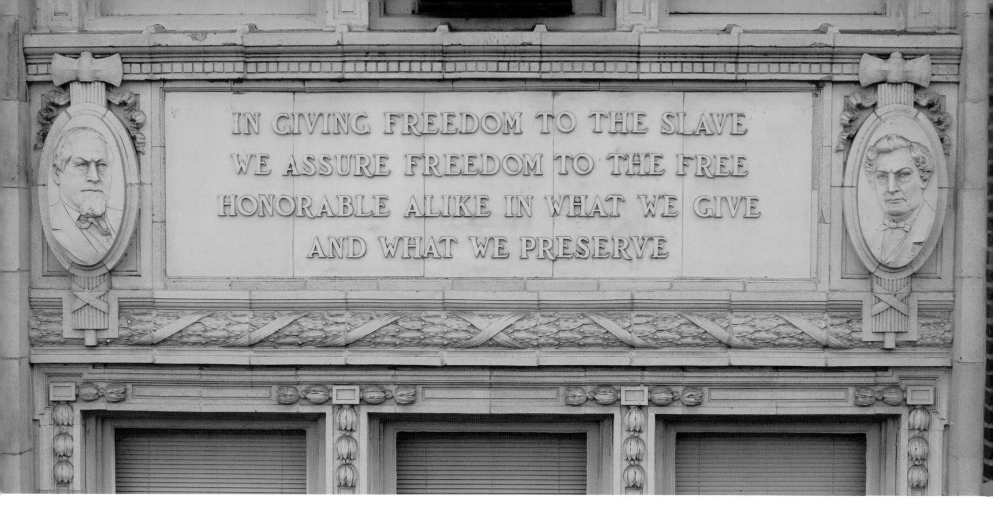

IN GIVING FREEDOM TO THE SLAVE
WE ASSURE FREEDOM TO THE FREE
HONORABLE ALIKE IN WHAT WE GIVE
AND WHAT WE PRESERVE

11. "My paramount object in this struggle is to save the Union, and is not either to save or to destroy slavery." Letter to Horace Greeley, Aug. 22, 1862 (*CW* 5:388). Lyman Trumbull (left) and Stephen A. Douglas (right).

12. "In giving freedom to the slave, we assure freedom to the free, honorable alike in what we give and what we preserve." Message to Congress, Dec. 1, 1862 (*CW* 5:537). John M. Palmer (left) and Richard Yates (right).

13. "The signs look better. The Father of Waters again goes unvexed to the sea. Thanks to the great Northwest for it." Letter to James C. Conkling, Aug. 26, 1863 (*CW* 6:409). Richard J. Oglesby (left) and John A. Logan (right).[5]

14. "That this nation, under God, shall have a new birth of freedom, and that government of the people, by the people, for the people, shall not perish from the earth." Gettysburg Address, Nov. 19, 1863 (*CW* 7:23). Owen Lovejoy (left) and Gustave Koerner (right).

15. "With malice toward none; with charity for all; with firmness in the right, as God gives us to see the right, let us strive on to finish the work we are in." Second Inaugural Address, Mar. 4, 1865 (*CW* 8:333). David Davis (left) and Joseph Medill (right).

16. "No men living are more worthy to be trusted than those who toil up from poverty, none less inclined to take, or touch, aught which they have not honestly earned." Message to Congress, Dec. 3, 1861 (*CW* 5:52–53).

17. "The man who stands by and says nothing when the peril of his government is discussed cannot be misunderstood." Letter to Erastus Corning and others, June 12, 1863 (*CW* 6:265).[6]

18. "It is upon the brave hearts and strong arms of the people of the country that our reliance has been placed in support of free government and free institutions." Speech to the Twelfth Indiana Regiment, May 13, 1862 (*CW* 5:213).

19. "The purposes of the Almighty are perfect and must prevail, though we erring mortals may fail to accurately perceive them in advance." Letter to Eliza P. Gurney, Sept. 4, 1864 (*CW* 7:535).[7]

20. "Judicial decisions are of greater or less authority as precedents according to circumstances." Speech at Springfield, June 26, 1857 (*CW* 2:401).

Many of these texts, especially those selected by Greene, are excerpted from some of Lincoln's best-known writings and are part of longer passages that are equally memorable. Other texts, such as numbers 5 and 12, are no less admirable, although in context they advance points regarding racial inequalities and colonization that jar modern sensibilities. And a few quotations, such as number 20, taken from a speech concerning the Dred Scott decision, are, standing alone, rather mundane.

PORTRAITS OF LINCOLN'S CONTEMPORARIES

Evarts B. Greene, who had suggested the Lincoln pictures and the Lincoln texts for the initial phase of construction, also drew up the list of contemporaries of Lincoln to portray in the medallions that were part of the building's terra cotta program. Greene in fact drew up two lists of prominent men in Lincoln's day, one for the nation and the other for Illinois. The portraits of those on the national list were placed on the south face of the building. Those on the Illinois list appear on the north face.

For Greene, as for others at the University, it was important to emphasize the contribution of the state to the nation. The Illinois portraits would also indicate the institution's position as the state University. Then, too, Lincoln Hall was funded through a legislative appropriation. As Greene declared, "Lincoln Hall, more definitely than any other building on the campus, is meant to express and emphasize the civic relations and obligations of the State University."[1]

In Greene's generation anyone familiar with American history was likely to recognize most of the figures portrayed on Lincoln Hall. Each portrait was based on a photograph, usually one taken during the Civil War. Of the twenty images, Greene's notes indicate that seven had been published in *Harper's Weekly*, five in Nicolay and Hay's *Abraham Lincoln: A History*, and the rest in a scattering of biographies and histories. Schneider, in rendering each likeness in relatively high relief, mainly used reproductions provided by Herbert Wells Fay, the photograph collector in DeKalb, but a few pictures came from descendants of those portrayed. For Jonathan Baldwin Turner, Greene turned to his daughter and biographer, Mary Turner Carriel, who had served on the University of Illinois Board of Trustees. She supplied a print from a daguerreotype of her father in 1853, "when he was lecturing on the university plan." Greene also contacted Lieutenant Governor John G. Oglesby for a picture of his father, Governor Richard J. Oglesby.[2]

Greene suggested that "the name of each person" be "attached to the medallion." Unfortunately, as American Terra Cotta's William Gates replied, this was "impossible as quite a number of portraits [were] already made," and Gates "[did] not see where to work in the name." Besides, he reasoned, "the portraits are so true that it will be unnecessary to label them."[3] If only Lincoln's contemporaries were known so well today!

Lincoln Hall's pantheon of national leaders, portrayed on the south side of the building, are, from left to right, the following men:

Horace Greeley, editor of the *New York Tribune*

Jonathan Baldwin Turner, educator

Charles Francis Adams, minister to Great Britain, 1861–68

Senator Charles Sumner of Massachusetts, 1851–74

Admiral David G. Farragut

General Ulysses S. Grant

Gideon Welles,
Secretary of the Navy,
1861–69

Edwin M. Stanton,
Secretary of War,
1861–68

Salmon P. Chase,
Secretary of the Treasury,
1861–64

William H. Seward,
Secretary of State,
1861–69

Representing Illinois on the north side of building, from left to right, are ten more men:

Senator Lyman Trumbull, 1855–73

Senator Stephen A. Douglas, 1847–61

Governor John M. Palmer, 1869–73

Governor Richard Yates, 1861–65

Governor Richard J. Oglesby, 1865–69, 1873, 1885–89

Major General
John A. Logan

Owen Lovejoy,
Member of Congress,
1857–64

Gustave Koerner,
Lieutenant Governor,
1853–57; Minister to
Spain, 1862–64

David Davis, Justice,
U.S. Supreme Court,
1862–76

Joseph Medill,
editor of the *Chicago
Tribune*

Writing to President James, Greene had no difficulty justifying most of those immortalized in the national group. Seward, Chase, Stanton, and Welles were the "heads of the four great federal departments" during the Civil War. Grant and Farragut represented "the military and naval service, respectively." Sumner was a leading legislator, while Adams represented "the diplomacy of the Civil War."[4]

James, however, did not accept Greene's suggestion of including Senator William Pitt Fessenden of Maine, who in 1864 succeeded Chase as Secretary of the Treasury. James preferred Greeley, probably the most prominent journalist of Lincoln's day. James did accept Greene's suggestion to include Jonathan Baldwin Turner, who, according to James, deserved "the real credit for originating the plan incorporated in the Land-Grant Act" to which the University owed its existence.[5]

Trumbull and Douglas, the state's two senators at the outset of the war, led off the Illinois side of Lincoln Hall. As Greene wrote to James, they were "clearly entitled to a place." Indeed, in the decade before the Civil War, Douglas was as conspicuous on the national stage as anyone on Greene's national list. Palmer, an early Republican leader and corps commander in the Civil War, was probably included because he later became a governor. "Yates," Greene wrote, "though in some respects open to criticism, was after all the war governor of the state." Greene felt no need to justify Oglesby, who followed Yates as governor. "The choice of Logan may

meet with some criticism," Greene noted, "but he was undoubtedly the most vigorous volunteer officer" from Illinois during the Civil War, and he was important in securing the loyalty of the southern part of the state. As a Democrat, he also helped balance Greene's list.[6]

Greene championed Owen Lovejoy, a member of Congress from northern Illinois, as "representative of the radical abolitionist attitude" of the state. Because Owen Lovejoy's brother Elijah, the Alton editor who was martyred in 1837 in the abolitionist cause, was perhaps better known than Owen, Greene took pains to see that the correct picture was used for the terra cotta portrait. In Greene's view, Gustave Koerner, active on Lincoln's behalf, was "perhaps the best representative of the German American element in the state" in the Civil War era. David Davis deserved recognition "because of his associations with Lincoln both as lawyer and as political lieutenant."[7]

James questioned the "claims" of Joseph Medill to a place among the Lincoln Hall portraits. Having himself prepared *A Bibliography of Newspapers Published in Illinois Prior to 1860* (1899), James thought that Charles H. Ray and Horace White, more than Medill, had guided the *Chicago Tribune* "during the civil war period" itself. Greene consulted with Franklin W. Scott, secretary of the Alumni Association, who had compiled *Newspapers and Periodicals of Illinois, 1814–1879* (1910). Scott gave his opinion of who was probably most important at the *Tribune*: Ray to 1863, White from 1864 to

1874, and then Medill, whose "chief claim to journalistic distinction rests on the long period during which he was potent in *Tribune* affairs." The choice, Scott concluded, "lies between Ray and Medill." Greene stuck with Medill, seeing him as important "in developing anti-slavery and union spirit in the north." To make this point, Greene noted that Medill had led a committee that asked Lincoln in 1864 to reduce Chicago's draft quota. The President had turned aside the request because, as Medill recalled in 1895, the *Tribune*'s anti-slavery stance had done much to bring on the war. Medill's recollection, one of several that "contributed more to the Lincoln myth than to Lincoln biography" (as two recent scholars have put it), was hardly the best evidence that Greene could have used, but no one else portrayed on Lincoln Hall received as much informed attention as did Medill.[8]

Greene on his own compiled the national list for James's review, withdrawing as he did so the name of General William T. Sherman. He evidently did not consider others, such as the abolitionists William Lloyd Garrison and Frederick Douglass, although his list as first drafted included Thaddeus Stevens.

In compiling the Illinois list, Greene sought the advice of others. Jessie Palmer Weber, in charge of the Illinois State Historical Library (and Governor Palmer's daughter), suggested Republican congressman Elihu B. Washburne, who championed Grant, and Wilbur F. Storey, editor of the *Chicago Times,* a Democratic paper

that opposed the war. Neither of these recommendations made the final cut. She also reported the views of others who had proposed William H. Bissell, the first Republican governor of the state, and Orville Hickman Browning, a Republican who took Douglas's seat in the Senate. Again, neither individual appeared on the building.

For German American names, Greene consulted Otto L. Schmidt, president of both the Illinois State Historical Society and the Chicago Historical Society. Dr. Schmidt proposed Gustave Koerner, the only one of Schmidt's suggestions to be adopted; Francis A. Hoffmann, lieutenant governor in the Yates administration; George Schneider, another Cook County Republican; "and especially George Bensen of Belleville," who was involved in shaping the state's first normal school (now Illinois State University).

Charles H. Rammelkamp, president of Illinois College, suggested Major General Benjamin H. Grierson, also a resident of Jacksonville; Peter Cartwright, the circuit rider and Democrat who ran for Congress against Lincoln; and Newton Bateman, state superintendent of public instruction. Paul Selby, who carried out Bateman's plan for combining the *Historical Encyclopedia of Illinois* with separate histories of nearly half the counties in the state, also proposed Bateman, and added Isaac Funk and James N. Brown, two agriculturalists. James Alton James, professor of history at Northwestern University, suggested John Wentworth, member of Congress and mayor of Chicago, and Thomas M. Eddy, another circuit rider, who edited the *Northwestern Christian Advocate* (Chicago) and compiled *The Patriotism of Illinois* (1865–66). Clark E. Carr, a leading Republican in Galesburg, remembered two Democrats who served in Congress, Major General John A. McClernand and James C. Robinson, who represented several eastern Illinois counties. None of these suggestions was adopted.

Joseph O. Cunningham, an Urbana editor and lawyer, observed that Greene had asked for leaders "not including Lincoln" from 1855 to 1865, whereas Lincoln and Douglas for the first half of that time were "the whole thing." After drawing up his own list of secondary figures, Cunningham noted that it did not include Richard Oglesby, a governor whose portrait was ultimately included on the building, or Shelby M. Cullom, who first went to Congress in 1865, because neither "was ever a leader, but both were cautious followers" only. Greene's notes point to two more discarded suggestions, Sidney Breese, U.S. Senator, 1843–49, and William H. Herndon, Lincoln's law partner.[9]

After considering all these nominations, Greene submitted his list of suggestions to President James, who deemed it "pretty satisfactory."[10] James spoke from solid knowledge of his own. He had published in the field of Illinois history and was one of three trustees of the Illinois State Historical Library until Greene took his place in 1911. Yet it was Greene, not James, who developed the list of leaders to depict on Lincoln Hall. Although Greene invited suggestions for the Illinois pantheon, he settled on figures who remain at the forefront of the state's history.

Greene was disappointed that a name could not be placed next to each portrait. Even in 1911, he had to intervene to be sure that the terra cotta company did not substitute Elijah Lovejoy's picture for Owen Lovejoy's or reverse the photographs of Palmer and Medill.[11]

A HOUSE DIVIDED AGAINST ITSELF
CANNOT STAND
I BELIEVE THIS GOVERNMENT CANNOT ENDURE
PERMANENTLY HALF SLAVE AND HALF FREE

LET US HAVE FAITH THAT RIGHT
MAKES MIGHT AND IN THAT FAITH
LET US TO THE END DARE TO DO
OUR DUTY AS WE UNDERSTAND IT

I HOLD THAT IN CONTEMPLATION OF
UNIVERSAL LAW AND OF THE CONSTITUTION
THE UNION OF THESE STATES IS PERPETUAL

WE ARE NOT ENEMIES BUT FRIENDS
WE MUST NOT BE ENEMIES
THOUGH PASSION MAY HAVE STRAINED
IT MUST NOT BREAK OUR BONDS OF AFFECTION

OTHER
EXTERIOR
DETAILS

HIGH UP on each facade of Lincoln Hall, under the cornice of the building, W. Carbys Zimmerman placed six escutcheons, four at the front corners of the building and one at the west end of each wing. With room for three names on each escutcheon, together the six escutcheons named eighteen Lincoln contemporaries. The names are now too tarnished to see clearly, but they carry out Evarts Greene's plan for the panels, with "national" figures on the south side of the building and "state" figures on the north.

Because there were ten pairs of portraits flanking the quotations, two of the twenty figures pictured on the building—Turner and Oglesby—went unnamed in the original escutcheons. The disparity was reversed when Lincoln Hall was extended to Wright Street in the late 1920s. James White, the campus architect who had supervised the building's initial construction, moved the escutcheons on each side to the corner of the addition and placed four more escutcheons on the new Wright Street facade. White retained the escutcheon design on the new facade. The addition included space for a dozen more names, but the medallions next to the new quotations were left blank. As a consequence, Lincoln Hall was completed with the names of thirty leaders on the escutcheons but portraits of only twenty on the panels.

Greene prepared the list of eighteen names for the six original shields on the front and sides of the building. This same list, to which Turner and Oglesby were added, was also used for the portraits next to the Lincoln texts. Thus the escutcheons provided a place elsewhere on the building for all of the names, even though that did little to identify the portraits.

The following names, read from the left starting on the south face, are inscribed on the escutcheons:

Adams, Sumner, Greeley
Welles, Grant, Farragut
Seward, Chase, Stanton
Douglas, Trumbull, Yates
Lovejoy, Koerner, Palmer
Davis, Medill, Logan[1]

For the Wright Street facade, White did not duplicate the front's flat facade but designed a pavilion at each end. These extensions allowed for four new escutcheons,

An escutcheon under the eave at each corner of the building shows the head of a lion at the top and three names on the shield below. In this pair of escutcheons, Seward, Chase, and Stanton are on the left (from the south side) and Douglas, Trumbull, and Yates are on the right (from the north side).

giving space for a dozen new names. The names appear again in groups of three. From the north to the south end of the west facade, the names are as follows:

Blair, Browning, Speed
Sheridan, McClernand, Fessenden
Turner, Sherman, Oglesby
Baker, Johnson, Hamlin

History professor Theodore Pease, who had proposed most of the Lincoln quotations for the new panels on the west half of the building, also gave White suggestions for most of the new names for the additional escutcheons. Only six men had not previously been considered:

Montgomery Blair, Postmaster General, 1861–64
Joshua Speed
Major General Philip Sheridan
Senator Edward D. Baker of Oregon, 1860–61
Vice President Andrew Johnson, 1865
Vice President Hannibal Hamlin, 1861–65

It is interesting that Pease proposed Joshua Speed, Lincoln's close friend in Springfield and later a Kentucky Unionist, rather than his brother James Speed, who succeeded Edward Bates as Attorney General in Lincoln's cabinet. Pease also introduced Baker, another friend, for whom the Lincolns named their second boy. And he suggested Sheridan, "if you want to commemorate another soldier."[2]

AT THE OUTSET of the project, Zimmerman designed a grand terra cotta doorway for the building. He crowned the entrance with a balustrade in line with the third floor and placed the words "Lincoln Hall" on the frieze, the years of Lincoln's life on the pendants, and a circular light on the level of the second floor. He added a decorative cartouche to the doorway itself and framed the steps into the building by ornamental lights.

For each secondary entrance, on the north and the south sides of the building, Zimmerman provided a simple terra cotta hood. Above each pair of doors would go a monogram he designed combining the letters "L" and "H" to signify *Lincoln Hall.* Later, above the entrances on Wright Street, White spelled out the name of the building and added decorative details and a monogram of his own, and he used the monogram again on the building's porte-cochere.

Zimmerman called upon Kristian Schneider to design one final detail for Lincoln Hall's exterior. Cast into the top of each of the mullions that separate the windows of the first floor is the head of a "wise old owl"—fifty-six altogether. Schneider also designed the eagles over "1809" and "1865" at the front entrance.[3]

One of the pair of lampposts that frame
the front entrance.

The main portal of Lincoln Hall leaves no doubt visually as to where to enter the building.

Over each side door of Lincoln Hall
Zimmerman overlapped the letters
"L" and "H" to form a monogram.
White simplified it for the doors
of the addition and in each arch of
the porte-cochere on Wright Street.

Employing an architectural conceit
of ancient vintage, Zimmerman and
White placed small owls' heads on
the mullions that separated Lincoln
Hall's first-floor windows.

Schneider designed the eagles over Lincoln's birth and death dates at the front entrance.

Above the entrances on Wright Street, White spelled out the name of the building and added decorative details.

LINCOLN HALL'S
MEMORIAL HALL

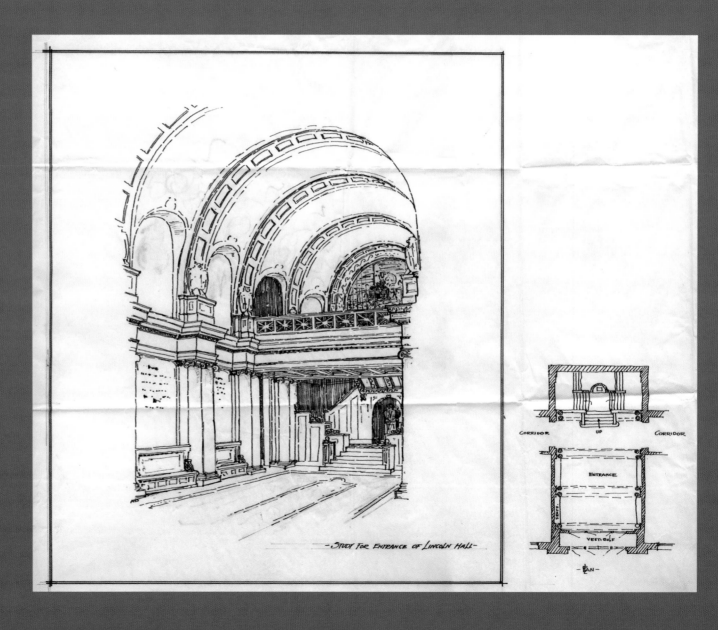

-Study for Entrance of Lincoln Hall-

CORRIDOR   UP   CORRIDOR

ENTRANCE

VESTIBULE

-PLAN-

THE ARTISTIC PROGRAM of Lincoln Hall included the interior as well as the exterior of the building. In 1909, Zimmerman planned "a handsome vestibule and entrance hall," a "Memorial Hall in honor of our great President," that would be "elaborately finished in marble and ornamental plaster." For this space, Greene proposed "a relief portrait of Lincoln done by a thoroughly competent artist, together with a tablet inscribed with selections from Lincoln's writings." Zimmerman noted how such suggestions could readily be accommodated, for the "wall spaces, recesses and other features" in his initial sketch were there "for the very purpose of inscriptions, statuary, tablets, etc."[1]

By 1911, discussion focused on a single Lincoln text for the entry hall. "What would you think," Greene asked President James, "of the propriety of using the Gettysburg address for this purpose?" It "appears so frequently" that critics may object, "but this address is so distinctly Lincoln's masterpiece that it seems hardly worth while to try to be original in our choice." Aware of the slight variations in the text of the several copies in Lincoln's hand, Greene asked

for the advice of a Lincoln authority, Daniel Kilham Dodge, professor of English. Dodge had edited *Lincoln's Inaugurals, Addresses and Letters* (1910) and had made "a very minute study of this subject."[2]

Where should Lincoln's words be placed? Greene, after discussing the matter with several colleagues as well as with James, felt that there would be "no impropriety" in placing the address on the floor. White was doubtful, proposing instead that it be a wall tablet. Zimmerman concurred: "This immortal saying should not be stepped upon." If something were to go on the floor, he suggested using "the book, plow, engine, etc." of the University seal. James wavered. In the end, however, he overruled Zimmerman. The Gettysburg Address would be "most easily read" on the floor; "more people" would "become familiar with it" there than anywhere else. The tablet itself, about five feet square, was cast in bold block letters by the F. P. Smith Wire and Iron Works, an ornamental iron and bronze company in Chicago, after Greene had it "strike out all commas, semicolons, and dashes" and a stray period in the first sentence.[3]

Zimmerman emphasized the vaulting in this study for the entrance of Lincoln Hall. He also included a niche, at the center of the staircase, that later accommodated a bust of Lincoln. Between the columns that support the ribs of the vaulting he provided room for Lincoln quotations, but only the Gettysburg Address was eventually placed there. Crowning each column, Zimmerman sketched a rather large owl, a traditional symbol of wisdom.

The text was laid into the floor of Memorial Hall shortly after the building was open, but nothing was immediately done to carry out Greene's proposal that the space also include a Lincoln portrait. However, Spierling & Linden, a Chicago firm, was engaged to finish the hall by painting the walls with four coats of "pure white lead and oil, tinted to such tones as will best harmonize with the marble columns and wainscot," and likewise by painting the vaulted ceiling with four coats, with "a border ornament in gold leaf and color."[4]

Zimmerman's coffered ceiling extends from the main entrance of Lincoln Hall to the staircase between the first and second floors. The staircase approaches the niche for the Lincoln bust, divides as it passes the niche, and ends at the bridge over the entry hall.

The niche at the end of the Memorial Hall accommodated Hermon Atkins MacNeil's bust of Lincoln.

Zimmerman placed a cartouche on the capital of each column in the Memorial Hall. The columns were so spaced that he was able to tuck ten owls into the sides of the cartouches.

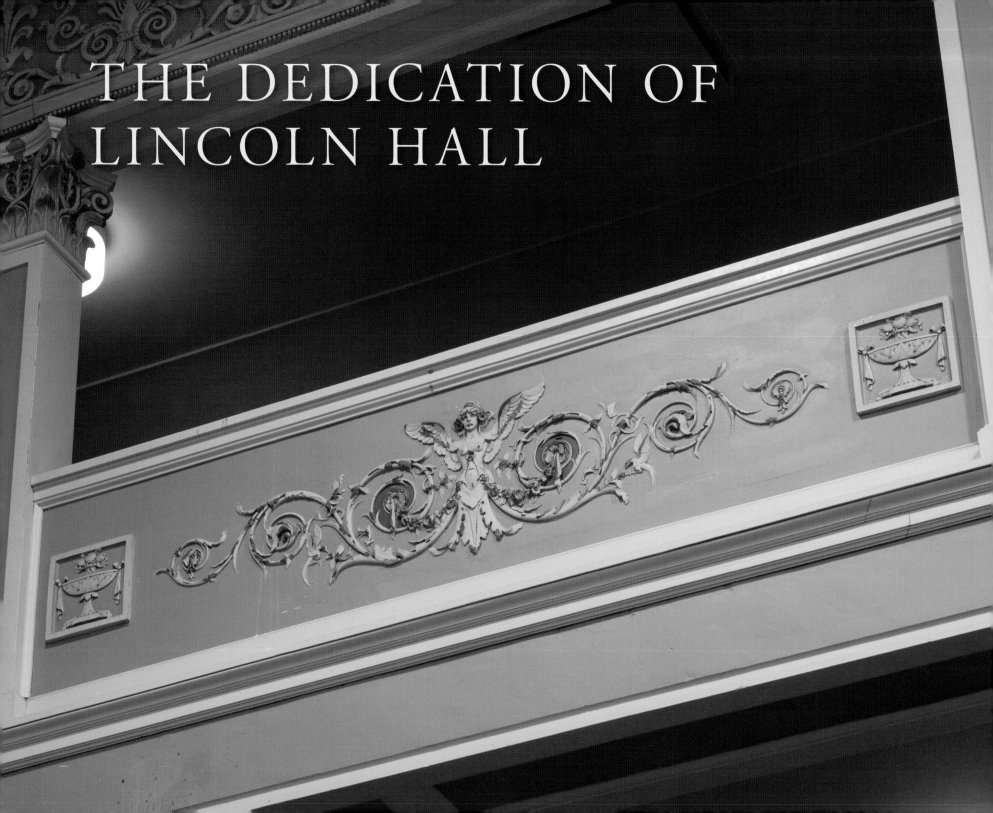

THE DEDICATION OF
LINCOLN HALL

During the summer of 1911, as Evarts Greene worked out plans for moving into Lincoln Hall in the fall, he also convened a committee to consider arrangements for the dedication of the building. Reflecting President James's expansive style, Greene at first proposed a three-day program. It would begin with addresses by nationally prominent professors in "history and politics, philology, literature, and philosophy," and "economic and social science"—fields that were to be centered in Lincoln Hall—and it would end with a conference led by several university presidents on the "Arts Courses in American Universities." The building itself would be formally dedicated on the middle day at a convocation to which hundreds of prominent figures would be invited. Greene's "Illinois List" included categories of people to invite such as legislators, state officials, the Illinois delegation in Congress, the state's newspaper editors, heads of Illinois colleges and normal schools, and professors in the relevant departments of those institutions. Greene also sketched out a "National List" along similar lines. He suggested, for instance, that the roster of "Presidents of State Universities and other principal colleges" be "more inclusive" for the West than for the East. And he proposed inviting "conspicuous surviving contemporaries of Lincoln (Horace White, J. G. Nicolay etc.)."[1]

Following James's suggestion, Greene collected the names of "descendants of the men whose names or medallions appear[ed] in the decoration" of Lincoln Hall. The dedication would provide an opportunity to bring to campus the families of those commemorated by the portraits and escutcheons on the building. James himself extended an invitation to Robert Todd Lincoln. Expressing his "gratification at such a monument being erected to the memory" of his father, the son carefully explained that he was not well, and accordingly was not only giving up his business affairs (including the presidency of the Pullman Palace Car Company) but also avoiding "any large assemblages, even operatic and theatrical performances." If his health improved, however, he would attend the dedication, if he could do so "without being expected to take any public part" in it. He took the same position in 1922, when he was present, but did not speak, at the dedication of the Lincoln Memorial in Washington, D.C.[2]

James next invited President William Howard Taft to speak at the dedication of Lincoln Hall. Lincoln had signed the Land Grant Act of 1862, "out of which the University of Illinois has grown," James wrote, "and we therefore look upon him as in a certain sense the founder of the institution." Lincoln had completed the legislation proposed by Jonathan B. Turner, "an ex–Yale man" (like Taft). James suggested that Lincoln and Turner had provided material for the President to weave into "an interesting, stimulating and provocative address upon the subject of federal aid to education." To reinforce his invitation, James turned to a number of influential Illinoisans who contacted the White House, including Governor Charles S. Deneen, Representative James R. Mann, Senator William B. McKinley, and Senator Shelby M. Cullom. But Taft, as his secretary explained, was unavailable. Senator Cullom summed up his own experience: "I went to see the President two or three times and failed. He was writing vetoes or holding cabinet meetings all the time, or something of that sort."[3]

Because Governor Deneen, who would be expected to speak at the dedication, was a Republican, it was thought necessary to pair him with "a prominent member of the Democratic party." Greene proposed Governor Woodrow Wilson of New Jersey, but the future President wrote that he was "obliged to decline all further engagements out of the State."[4]

Early in September 1911, it was decided to postpone "the dedicatory exercises" due to "unexpected complications." Evidently, the primary reason for postponing the dedication was the failure of the American Terra Cotta Company to complete its work. Throughout the summer, Greene and Zimmerman attempted to hasten it along, but Gates could only plead in reply that the job had been delayed a month in response to objections that the panels should not be mounted so far above the ground. When that tempest had passed, Kristian Schneider, as Gates explained, was so occupied with other work that he could not complete the Lincoln Hall order on schedule. Gates tried "to get extra modellers" for other jobs, thus letting Schneider finish up the panels, but this proved impossible. Even if Lincoln Hall were to take Schneider's "exclusive time," he still would be unable to complete on time more than five of "the pictorial panels." Although Gates was "really sorry that we got into this tangle," it had the effect of canceling the dedication in 1911.[5]

Not until August 1912 did American Terra Cotta ship the last of the panels. When every panel had been put it place, two of the recast inscriptions, which had been incorrectly numbered, had to be reversed so as to maintain the chronological order Greene wanted.[6]

Late in 1912, James again began to plan "dedicatory exercises" for Lincoln Hall. He decided "to limit the program to a single day," Lincoln's birthday in 1913. Accordingly, he arranged for three addresses in the morning: Frederick Woodbridge, professor of philosophy at Columbia University; Bliss Perry, professor of English literature at Harvard University; and Albert Shaw, editor of the American monthly *Review of Reviews.* The three men spoke, respectively, on philosophical studies, language and literature, and the social sciences. For the afternoon ceremony, James scheduled the Reverend Hugh Black, professor of practical theology at Union Theological Seminary, who spoke on Lincoln. Next, Edward F. Dunne, the state's newly elected governor, formally transferred the building to the University. "We are here today," Dunne declared, "to announce officially the consummation of a great educational edifice" and to unveil "another great monument" to Lincoln, who, by signing the Land-Grant Act, was "the greatest philanthropist of his age."[7]

Publicity in the press about the dedication led at least two individuals to propose additions to the program, both of which were politely declined. A professor of Greek at Marietta College in Ohio offered to recite an ode he had written, and a Chicago physician suggested that "some colored man represent his race" at the dedication. "To ten million citizens of color in the republic," Dr. Leonard W. Lewis wrote, Lincoln was "preeminently" the Emancipator. "We need now a second emancipation, one to free us from the shackles of race prejudice, to make us free industrially and otherwise." Lewis offered to make this "plea for a second emancipation" himself. Lewis, born in Champaign and educated in the town's high school and at Fisk University, had "spent many hours beneath the shadow of Lincoln's tomb," where he had "received inspiration to do and to be."[8]

In preparing for the rescheduled dedication, James again unsuccessfully urged Robert Todd Lincoln to attend. He also invited the descendants of those memorialized in terra cotta on the building, the heirs of Owen Lovejoy and Joseph Medill being the most numerous. He proposed an exhibit of "some of our Lincoln material," to which he fondly hoped to add the autobiography Lincoln wrote at the request of Jesse Fell, a Bloomington lawyer, town promoter, and politician. But the invitation to Fell's daughters did not yield that priceless document, now in the Library of Congress, although the University later acquired Fell's commission as paymaster, signed by Lincoln.[9]

Invitations to the dedication also had gone out to various colleges and universities and to newspaper editors. James cancelled classes so that every student could attend the day's proceedings, and faculty were invited to appear in academic attire at the afternoon convocation in the Auditorium. James directed that all University buildings and laboratories be closed during the program, which was evidently well attended. But relatively few out-of-town guests came for the day. The luncheon was served to only 162 persons, 80 of whom were "members of the faculty who paid for their tickets." Nothing, however, could diminish James's enthusiasm for Lincoln Hall. "You ought to come out and see our building," he wrote to a friend at Yale shortly after the dedication. "It is really the finest monument thus far erected to Abraham Lincoln in the country," he remarked, although, as he added with a touch of humor, the Lincoln Memorial in the Capital would "soon throw us into the shade."[10]

Meanwhile, Greene gave up his post as dean of Literature and Arts, effective February 1, 1913. James asked Arthur H. Daniels, a professor of philosophy who became acting dean, to handle arrangements for the dedication. Before the dedication, however, Greene prepared for publication a description of Lincoln Hall, giving attention both to the departmental arrangements within the building and to the building's commemorative program. Greene's text, which made no reference to his own role in shaping the historical dimension of Lincoln Hall's art, was published as a booklet with and without illustrations.[11] In both, Greene included a Lincoln text that seemed to fit a building for the humanities. Acknowledging in 1864 an honorary degree from the College of New Jersey (Princeton University), Lincoln had written: "I am most thankful if my labors have seemed to conduce to the preservation of those institutions under which alone we can expect good government and in its train sound learning and the progress of the liberal arts."[12]

FROM THE CENTENNIAL
TO THE BICENTENNIAL

The University community welcomed the construction of Lincoln Hall, which not only accommodated departments that had been crammed into the old University Hall (on the site of the present Illini Union) but also contributed to the development of the space, terminated by the Auditorium, that would become the Quad. Students were apparently so eager to use the departmental libraries that they picked the locks on the doors after hours![1]

The success of Lincoln Hall was also signified by the construction nearby of two new campus landmarks. The Class of 1912 placed, at the northeast corner of the building, a stone, semicircular Roman bench around a Doric column, and the Class of 1913 donated a Georgian brick and stone gateway at the southwest corner of the building. Earlier class gifts included a bench, a sundial, and a fountain, but none contributed so directly to the setting of a campus building. A less conspicuous class gift was later placed within the confines of Lincoln Hall itself. In 1968, the Classes of 1918 and 1919 funded a war memorial in the south courtyard of the building.

For many years after Lincoln Hall opened in 1911, the niche at the end of Memorial Hall was empty. In 1923, however, supervising architect James White took up Greene's initial suggestion that a portrait of Lincoln take that place of honor. He wrote to Lorado Taft, a leading sculptor of the day who maintained close ties with the University, his alma mater. At the suggestion of Daniel Kilham Dodge, White asked Taft if a copy of Gutzon Borglum's massive head of Lincoln might serve the purpose. Taft replied: "I regret to say that Borglum's so called 'Lincoln' is my pet aversion; I would prefer not to help in this matter."[2]

Undeterred, White asked Taft what he might suggest, and the sculptor evidently proposed a work of his own: "My marble-cutter thinks that a bust of the size proposed" could be executed for $500, half "for the marble (Serravezza)" and half for the cutting. "I would be glad to provide the model without cost." White, after conferring with University president David Kinley, assured Taft that Kinley was confident he could obtain the money "from outside sources."[3]

The Class of 1912 located a stone bench and column between Lincoln Hall and what is now the English Building. Photographers have ever since used such class gifts as a setting.

The Class of 1913 placed a gateway to the campus near Wright Street. In the background is the original part of Lincoln Hall, before the addition brought the building closer to the gateway.

the niche Sunday for the purpose of demonstration."[4] Taft completed the statue, now in Urbana's Carle Park, but his bust for Lincoln Hall did not materialize. Rather, the University acquired a Lincoln bust made by Taft's friend Hermon Atkins MacNeil.

An instructor at Cornell and at the Art Institute of Chicago, MacNeil achieved renown for his sculptures of Native Americans and large-scale memorial statues. In 1914, he was invited to participate in a competition to design a statue of Lincoln for the front of the Illinois State Capitol. The competition was won by Andrew O'Connor, whose statue was dedicated in 1918. In an issue of the *Art World* that year, F. Wellington Ruckstull published a photograph of MacNeil's plaster model of "Lincoln the Lawyer," with the subject posed as if he were about to examine a witness or address a jury. Ruckstull also described MacNeil's Lincoln as a politician on the stump, referring in particular to Lincoln's appearance in Petersburg during the Frémont campaign of 1856, when Lincoln patiently waited for a hostile Democratic crowd to settle down before he spoke. In his five-foot-high model, MacNeil gave Lincoln a confident stance, with arms folded across his chest, an almost unique pose in Lincoln sculpture. Somewhat incongruously, MacNeil placed a bench behind Lincoln on which he had carelessly thrown his coat and hat. The bench itself was decorated by a stately eagle, pointing to the presidency.[5]

Taft praised MacNeil's work for its "dependable sanity" amid "the eccentricities and vagaries of current endeavor." MacNeil had "never exemplified this quality

Two years later, Taft had turned his attention to a Lincoln statue in Urbana, secured "through the generosity of Judge and Mrs. J. O. Cunningham, personal friends of Abraham Lincoln." According to the *Daily Illini,* Taft was scheduled to come to town to show "a few pictures of how the statue will look when it is completed. . . . Prof. Taft is also making a bust of Lincoln for the niche in Lincoln hall, and will place a model of it in to better advantage than in his fine 'Lincoln' model, a work meriting enlargement and a prominent place." But the plaster model was never turned into full-size bronze statue. The most that MacNeil ever did was to sculpt a bust of a quiet, contemplative Lincoln, again with folded arms, this time resting on a simple plinth. Evidently, eight copies were cast and consigned to Grand Central Art Galleries in New York City, which sent one copy on approval to the University of Illinois. The Trustees bought it for $450, drawing on the Reserve and Contingent Fund.[6]

MacNeil's bust, mounted on a marble pedestal in 1929, presented its subject with skill and sensitivity. Indeed, it may be regarded as the most accomplished contribution to Lincoln art in Lincoln Hall. Students soon began to rub Lincoln's nose for good luck.

The tablet containing the words of the Gettysburg Address fared less well. The question that had divided administrators and architects in 1911—whether to embed it in the floor or mount it on a wall—persisted as a debatable point for the next forty-odd years. Shortly after the building's dedication, the Council of Administration heard student objections to the "unsuitable" location of the tablet. In 1921, when the American Legion entered the dispute, the Trustees instructed White to place the sacred words elsewhere. But he declared that the tablet could not "be removed without destroying it. Would not the purpose be accomplished by putting a light bronze rail around it?" The Trustees rescinded their action and asked President Kinley to notify the Legion.[7]

Letters regarding the tablet and the respect it was due soon became a staple in the *Daily Illini*. Was it to be trod upon as if it were a "doormat"? Should students be allowed to "congregate on the plate, laughing and talking, and idly twisting their heels as though trying to erase the lettering of a masterpiece of the English language"? Would not the "constant shuffling and scrapping of feet" across the tablet cause it to look "like the very hell in a very short time"?[8]

It soon became a University tradition that the sacred words were not to be "profaned" by walking on them. Students monitored traffic through the hall and tabulated how many disregarded "one of the best known and most respected traditions of Illinois." Men and women were "equally guilty" of failing to step around the tablet, but those who were most culpable were new to the University. "It takes about a year to have the incoming class told that the tablet is sacred and by that time another unschooled group of students is here." But hardened violators regarded the tradition as "foolish," one of the "time-honored quirks and oddities" of the campus, and even a ploy to cover up the administration's "error" in placing the tablet on the floor.[9]

The administration eventually pulled up the worn-down tablet and mounted it on the south wall of the entry hall. Apparently because the tablet had been made for the floor, its design was plain and utilitarian, without typographical elegance—characteristics that became more obvious when it was installed on the wall.

From his plaster statue of Lincoln, MacNeil modeled a bronze bust, a copy of which the university acquired in 1928 for the niche at the entrance to Lincoln Hall. Students going to classes in Lincoln Hall's large auditorium use the stairs next to the Lincoln bust—and they polish the nose as they pass.

Hermon Atkins MacNeil sculpted a full-size statue of Lincoln for a competition in 1914. The work, apparently now lost, was pictured in an art periodical in 1918, but it is generally unknown to Lincoln specialists.

Embedded for decades in the floor of the entrance to Lincoln Hall, the tablet containing the words of the Gettysburg Address was eventually mounted on a wall near the door. The bronze letters of the Gettysburg Address, although worn down by their years on the floor, are still readable on the wall.

FOURSCORE AND SEVEN [ ] A NEW NATION

FORTH ON THIS CONTINENT A NEW NATION

LIBERTY AND DEDICATED TO THE PROPOSITION

ARE CREATED EQUAL.

NOW WE ARE ENGAGED IN A GREAT CIVIL

WHETHER THAT NATION OR ANY NATION SO

O DEDICATED CAN LONG ENDURE. WE ARE ME

ATTLE FIELD OF THAT WAR. WE HAVE COME

PORTION OF THAT FIELD AS A FINAL REST

HOSE WHO HERE GAVE THEIR LIVES THAT

IGHT LIVE. IT IS ALTOGETHER FITTING AND

E SHOULD DO THIS.

BUT IN A LARGER SENSE WE CANNOT DEDICA

NSECRATE WE CANNOT HALLOW THIS GROUN

President David Kinley. Toward the end of his tenure, 1920–1930, he initiated the completion of Lincoln Hall according to the original plan of 1909.

THE 1909 PLANS for Lincoln Hall provided for an addition to the original building. This addition became a priority by 1926 "because of the rapid growth of the College of Liberal Arts and Sciences." The campus's "greatest need" was "for fairly centrally located class room space." Accordingly, in 1927, the Trustees earmarked in the legislature's biennial appropriation to the University $500,000 for "the completion of Lincoln Hall."[10]

James M. White, still the supervising architect on campus, promptly drew up plans for the "West Wing of Lincoln Hall." Except in detail, these plans duplicated the original structure he and Zimmerman had designed. Hunzinger & Company of Davenport, Iowa, became the general contractor, underbidding English Brothers of Champaign.[11]

When Lincoln Hall was doubled in size and the addition was connected almost seamlessly to the old part, the building was used in substantially different ways. White, explaining his plans to President Kinley, wrote that Lincoln Hall, having "served its purpose as a building for graduate study," was to become "the undergraduate headquarters for work in Liberal Arts." In 1928 and 1929, classrooms and offices came to occupy most of the space on the three principal floors, while the departmental libraries and seminar rooms, intended for advanced studies, were moved to the new University library that was displacing the orchard to the south of Lincoln Hall.[12]

In its early years, Lincoln Hall was home to many departments: Classics, Philosophy, Psychology, and Education on the first floor, English and Modern Languages on the second, and History, Political Science, Economics, and Sociology on the third. Later, as the University grew, several units migrated to adjacent buildings: for example, English moved into what had been the Woman's Building (1905, with additions in 1913 and 1924), and History and Philosophy moved to Gregory Hall, built in 1939.

During the expansion of Lincoln Hall and for many years after, the fourth floor was less changed. Research centers such as the Illinois Historical Survey retained their rooms in the attic of the original building; the survey did not move to the library until 1966. The addition to Lincoln Hall did give much more space to the Museum of Classical Archaeology and Art on the south side and the Museum of European Culture on the north side of the building's fourth floor. The two museums, renamed the World Heritage Museum in 1971, migrated to the Spurlock Museum in 2002.

In the courtyard enclosed by the addition, White designed a large lecture hall. For many decades, it also served as the principal theatrical venue on campus.

Lincoln Hall was completed by the construction in the courtyard of a large lecture hall, designed to seat about 750 people. White also planned for the hall to serve as a theater. Although the Department of Psychology wanted the space for a laboratory, and Kinley at first favored the idea, the department had to wait until 1969 for its own building. Drawing on an Illini Theatre Guild fund and the Trustees' appropriations for stage equipment, stage lighting, and "ornamental plaster," White decorated the niches and walls of the lecture hall and theater with Adamesque panels, niches, and medallions. For better access to the entire building, White added a porte-cochere on Wright Street.[13]

The niches on either side of the stage were used for stage lighting.

White ornamented the lecture hall with garlands, medallions, and panels in a style reminiscent of the late eighteenth-century neoclassical designs of Robert Adam and his brothers.

Stylized griffins are prominent in the panels next to the stage.

The vaulted ceiling of the lobby outside the lecture hall was also ornamented.

The porte-cochere on the Wright Street side provided a touch of elegance to the building. For many years it was a functional amenity, giving performers direct access to the stage door of the lecture hall.

On the exterior, White extended the terra cotta panels so as to accommodate ten more Lincoln quotations. To cast the panels, he turned to American Terra Cotta, the same company that had provided panels for the original building. In 1928, William Gates was semiretired. Fritz Wagner Jr. (Illinois Class of 1908) was now president and was in a position to see that the format and lettering of the new panels were the same as in the old ones.[14] Yet there was one conspicuous change: the medallions on each new panel were left bare. Evidently no one proposed that they be filled with more portraits. The golden age of terra cotta craftsmanship had passed.

THE ART ON THE BUILDING'S EXTERIOR has not weathered the years in a uniform way. With photographs of Lincoln's contemporaries to copy for the portrait medallions, Schneider cast the portraits in high relief. In 1912, Gates proudly noted that the portraits were so skillfully modeled that even the spectacles worn by Greeley and Stanton were clearly visible.[15] The medallions' bold, simple lines have stood up fairly well. Similarly, the inscriptions on each side of the building, cast in simple block letters, have retained their readability.

The passage of time has taken a greater toll on the panels that document Lincoln's life. Schneider, with little pictorial evidence to draw upon, developed each scene in such shallow relief that some details are no longer visible. Moreover, water has damaged and cracked those panels more than the terra cotta elsewhere on the building. Schneider's life of Lincoln was never easy to see because the panels were so white and so elevated. Set against white terra cotta window frames, the panels "blend in so well you may not see them," as Edward J. Hynds Jr. recently said. Yet Hynds, who heads English Brothers today, opined that Lincoln Hall's terra cotta, as a whole, has "held up amazingly well."[16]

The same cannot be said of the escutcheons on the building. After eighty or more years, the names on those copper shields have become so tarnished as to be virtually unreadable (see p. 72). Lincoln Hall no longer provides by name a tribute to the thirty Lincoln contemporaries who were once so prominent.

Architectural terra cotta was a much-favored building material a century ago. Used extensively on Lincoln Hall, it continues to give the building distinction today. The architects, W. Carbys Zimmerman and James M. White, gave the structure a stately presence that was particularly admired at the time. Evarts B. Greene provided the ideas and Kristian Schneider the craftsmanship that gave the building its special characteristics as a tribute to Lincoln. Greene took quiet pride in what they together had accomplished: "The whole makes a unique and successful attempt to use exterior decoration in terra cotta to emphasize the beauty and the dignity of a memorial building."[17]

Lincoln Hall's main entrance.

ACKNOWLEDGMENTS

FOR ADVICE AND ASSISTANCE in preparing this study of Lincoln Hall on the campus of the University of Illinois at Urbana-Champaign, I wish to acknowledge Melvyn A. Skvarla, architect and Campus Historic Preservation Officer in the Planning Division of the University's Office of Facilities and Services; Sharon S. Darling of St. Charles, Illinois, a decorative arts historian; Bryan Whitledge, who digitized photographs in the University Archives; and David B. Wiegers of Gurnee, Illinois, whose historical and architectural photography includes the Lincoln Sculpture Project. In addition, I am indebted to Kristine Campbell, Assistant Vice President for Academic Affairs, who advanced the project. The manuscript benefited from close readings by James Cornelius, Curator of the Lincoln Collection of the Abraham Lincoln Presidential Library, and my brother Donald Hoffmann, an architectural historian. Finally, I am grateful for Erin New's work in the design of the book and for the publication skills of the staff of the University of Illinois Press, including Willis G. Regier, director; Cope Cumpston, art director; and Jennifer L. Reichlin, editorial, design, and production manager.

NOTES

Foreword

1. "To the People of Sangamon County, Mar. 9, 1932," in *The Collected Works of Abraham Lincoln,* edited by Roy P. Basler; Marion Delores Pratt and Lloyd A. Dunlap, assistant editors. 9 vols. (New Brunswick, N.J.: Rutgers University Press, 1953–55), 1:8.

To Educate and Inspire

1. [Evarts B. Greene], *Lincoln Hall, University of Illinois* (Urbana?: University of Illinois, 1912?), 3.
2. Ibid., 3, 5; "Editorial," *Alumni Quarterly of the University of Illinois,* 6:1 (Jan. 1912), 16; "Lincoln Hall for the Humanities," *The Survey: A Journal of Constructive Philanthropy,* 29:18 (Feb. 1, 1913), 564. *The Survey*'s article was written by Graham Taylor, who had founded the Chicago Commons settlement. See Taylor to Edmund J. James, Feb. 19, 1913, University Archives, University of Illinois at Urbana-Champaign, James, General Correspondence, 1904–19, 2/5/3, Box 34, Lincoln Hall folders (hereafter 2/5/3, 34). Taylor referred to the expulsion from the U.S. Senate of William Lorimer of Chicago on charges that he had bought his seat. The Lorimer case hastened the ratification in 1913 of the Seventeenth Amendment to the Constitution, which provided for the direct election of U.S. senators.
3. "Scrip" [William D. Gates], "A New Life of Lincoln: A Most Wonderful Story Told in Terra Cotta," *The Clay-Worker,* 57:4 (Apr. 1912), 605.

Plans for Lincoln Hall

1. *Laws of the State of Illinois Enacted by the Forty-Sixth General Assembly* (Springfield: Illinois State Journal Co., 1910), 44–45.
2. James M. White to Evarts B. Greene, July 15, 1909, Project Files for Lincoln Hall, Records Office, Facilities and Services, Box 708, Evarts Greene file (hereafter 708, Greene [or another file]); W. Carbys Zimmerman to Edmund J. James, Aug. 31, 1909, James, General Correspondence, 1904–19, University Archives, 2/5/3, Box 22, Lincoln Hall folders (hereafter 2/5/3, 22).
3. Christine Des Garennes, "What's Next for Lincoln Hall?" *Champaign-Urbana News-Gazette,* Oct. 22, 2006, A-3, col. 4, citing Melvyn Skvarla, Historic Preservation Officer, University of Illinois. See also Zimmerman to James, Oct. 6, 1909, 2/5/3, 22; White to Zimmerman, Dec. 7, 1909; Zimmerman to White, Dec. 13, 1909; White to Zimmerman, Dec. 16, 1909, all in 708, Zimmerman.

4. Greene to James, Nov. 10, 1909; James to Zimmerman, Nov. 10, 1909; Zimmerman to James, Nov. 13, 1909, all in 2/5/3, 22; *Twenty-fifth Report (Seven Annual, Eighteen Biennial) of the Board of Trustees of the University of Illinois, Urbana, Illinois, for the Two Years Ending September 30, 1910* (Springfield: Illinois State Journal Co., 1911), 471–72 [hereafter cited as Board of Trustees, *25th Report* (or another number)].

5. James to Zimmerman, Dec. 29, 1909, 2/5/3, 22.

6. [Greene], "Notes on Discussion of New University Hall," Sept. 30, 1909; Greene to Zimmerman, Oct. 11, 1909; Greene to James, Mar. 12, 1910; Recommendations (for the consideration of the Board of Trustees) [Greene probably wrote the text; the interlineations are in Zimmerman's hand], n.d. but before Nov. 26, 1909; Endorsement on White to Greene, Apr. 11, 1911. See also Zimmerman to James, Sept. 14, 1909, Oct. 6, 1909, all in 2/5/3, 22.

7. White to Zimmerman, Mar. 18, 1910; James to Zimmerman, Mar. 18, 1910; Zimmerman to White, Mar. 21, 1910, all in 2/5/3, 22.

8. Greene to James, Mar. 3, 1910; James to Greene, n.d. (before Feb. 25, 1910), both in Literature and Arts Correspondence, 1899–1913, University Archives, 15/1/5, Box 7, Lincoln Hall folders (hereafter 15/1/5, 7); see White to James, Dec. 2, 1909; James to White, Feb. 1, 1910; White to James, Feb. 5, 1910, all in James, Faculty Correspondence, 1904–1915, University Archives, 2/5/6, Box 18, James M. White folders (hereafter 2/5/6, 18). White's long and distinguished career as supervising architect on campus was recognized by President David Kinley in *History of the Growth and Development of the Campus of the University of Illinois* by Leon Deming Tilton and Thomas Edward O'Donnell ([Urbana]: University of Illinois Press, 1930), ix, and in "James McLaren White," *Illinois Alumni News,* 11:6 (Mar. 1933), 188.

9. Zimmerman to William L. Abbott, Mar. 8, 1910, in Board of Trustees, *25th Report,* Mar. 9, 1910, 517; ibid., Apr. 12, 1910, 529.

10. James to White, n.d. [ca. Feb. 25, 1910], 2/5/6, 18. See also Greene to James, Feb. 25, 1910, University Archives, 2/5/6, Box 15 (hereafter 2/5/6, 15); White to Greene, Apr. 11, 1910, 2/5/6, 18.

11. Zimmerman to Greene, Nov. 8, 1910, 15/1/5, 7; "Lincoln Hall—Deductions," Item #7, n.d. but related to White to Greene, Apr. 11, 1910, 2/5/3, 22.1.

Planning Lincoln Hall's Lincoln Art

1. Zimmerman to James, Apr. 15, 1910, 708, James; James to Greene, Apr. 19, 1910, 15/1/5, 7; James to White, Apr. 19, 1910, 2/5/3, 22. See also James to Zimmerman, Apr. 19, 1910, 2/5/3, 22.

2. Greene to Zimmerman, May 25, 1910, 2/5/3, 22.

3. Greene to James, Sept. 26, 1910, 2/5/3, 22.

4. Theodore C. Pease, "Evarts Boutell Greene, 1870–1947," *Journal of the Illinois State Historical Society,* 41:1 (Mar. 1948), 13. See also Jack Randolph Kirby, "Evarts Boutell Greene: The Career of a Professional Historian" (Ph.D. diss., University of Illinois, 1969).

5. The house Greene lived in was then on the site of the Chapel of St. John the Divine but is now moved back from the corner.

Construction

1. Hopkins to White, May 22, 1910, and see Jensen to White, Jan. 24, 1910; Burrill to James, Jan. 20, 1910, all in 2/5/6, 18.

2. White to John B. Hutchings Jr., May 16, 1910, 2/5/6, 18; Board of Trustees, *26th Report,* Sept. 20, 1910, 22.

Making the Terra Cotta

1. [Edward C. English] to Zimmerman, Dec. 3, 1910, 2/5/3, 22.
2. George A. Berry III, with Sharon S. Darling, *Common Clay: A History of American Terra Cotta Corporation, 1881–1966* (Crystal Lake, Ill.: TCR Corp., 2003), 1, 17; Sharon S. Darling, *Chicago Ceramics and Glass: An Illustrated History from 1871 to 1933* (Chicago: Chicago Historical Society, 1979); Linda Garfield, "William Day Gates and the American Terra Cotta and Ceramic Company," *Historic Illinois,* 16:4 (Dec. 1993), 1–5, 14.
3. [William D. Gates], "Who's Who in the American Terra Cotta Co.," *Common Clay,* 1:4 (Oct. 1921), 13, reprinted in Berry, *American Terra Cotta,* 131; Sharon S. Darling, *Teco: Art Pottery of the Prairie School* (Erie, Pa.: Erie Art Museum, 1989), 175; Martin W. Reinhart, "Norwegian-Born Sculptor, Kristian Schneider: His Essential Contribution to the Development of Louis Sullivan's Ornamental Style," unpublished paper (1982), copy in Illinois History and Lincoln Collections, University of Illinois Library.

Other Terra Cotta Projects at Illinois

1. William Gray Purcell, undated note, quoted in Reinhart, "Norwegian-American Sculptor, Kristian Schneider," 19. For a discussion of the Stock Pavilion's medallions, see Elizabeth Campbell et al., "Building Condition Assessment and Restoration Proposal," an unpublished paper in the Preservation of Materials course (Architecture 419, Fall 2001), Sec. 3.1, copy in the Planning Division, Office of Facilities and Services, University of Illinois at Urbana-Champaign.
2. Board of Trustees, July 16, 1957, May 29, 1958, *49th Report,* 512, 1250–51.
3. Richard D. Mohr, "Art Ceramics at the University of Illinois-Urbana," *Journal of the American Art Pottery Association,* 13:6 (Nov.–Dec. 1997), 10–11.
4. Ibid., 11–12.

Lincoln's Life and Times in Terra Cotta

1. "Life of Lincoln," *The Clay-Worker,* 605–6; Lewis M. Gross, *Past and Present of DeKalb County, Illinois* (Chicago: Pioneer Publishing, 1907), 1:386–90; Zimmerman to Fay, Sept. 11, 1911, and see Gates to Greene, Sept. 15, 1911, both in University Archives, 15/1/5, Box 10, Lincoln Hall folders (hereafter 15/1/5, 10).
2. Gates to Zimmerman, Aug. 14, 1911; Zimmerman to Greene, Aug. 14, 1911 (see also Greene to Zimmerman, Aug. 10, 1911); [Greene], "Memorandum of the Assignment of Departmental Quarters in Lincoln Hall, July, 1911," all in 2/5/3, 22.
3. Unless otherwise noted, quotations regarding the panels depicting Lincoln's life and times in terra cotta are in Greene to Zimmerman, May 25, 1910, 2/5/3, 22, and in "A New Life of Lincoln," *The Clay-Worker,* 57:4 (Apr. 1912), 605–10. See also *Common Clay,* 1:1 (July 1920), 8–9, reprinted in Berry, *American Terra Cotta,* 95.
4. Greene to Albert Moore Saxe (in Zimmerman's office), Apr. 20, 1911; Greene to American Terra Cotta and Ceramic Company, May 2, 1911; and see [Franklin W. Scott],

memorandum regarding "the best writers" on this subject, all in 15/1/5, 7. See also Philip Shaw Paludan, "Lincoln and Negro Slavery: I Haven't Got Time for the Pain," *Journal of the Abraham Lincoln Association,* 27:2 (Summer 2006), 1–23.

5. William H. Herndon and Jesse William Weik, *Herndon's Lincoln,* ed. Douglas L. Wilson and Rodney O. Davis (Urbana: University of Illinois Press, 2006), 213. Also see *Thomas v. Wright,* in *The Law Practice of Abraham Lincoln,* Ser. I of *The Papers of Abraham Lincoln* (Springfield: Illinois Historic Preservation Agency, 2000; second edition, online at www.papersofabrahamlincoln.org, 2009); Paul H. Verduin, "A New Lincoln Discovery: Rebecca Thomas, His 'Revolutionary War Widow,'" *Lincoln Herald,* 98:1 (Spring 1996), 3–11.

6. See Edwin Erle Sparks, ed., *The Lincoln-Douglas Debates of 1858* (Springfield: Illinois State Historical Library, 1908). For Gates and Schneider, it was the Lincoln-Douglas Debate (in the singular).

A Smaller Set of Panels

1. "Terra Cotta Factory News," *Crystal Lake Herald,* Dec. 16, 1920, and Jan. 21, 1921 (clippings courtesy of Sharon S. Darling, St. Charles, Illinois, in the curatorial files of the Macon County Historical Society, Patrick McDaniel, executive director).

2. *Herndon's Lincoln,* ed. Wilson and Davis, 60.

Praise and Criticism

1. Gates, "A New Life of Lincoln," 8–9. Gates, however, was also realistic. Throughout his writings, he not only celebrated

terra cotta as impervious to water but also cautioned that water would break down the mortar between the panels and the intricate work that held them in place. Thus, to prevent serious damage, terra cotta installations required periodic attention.

2. Greene, "The Meaning of Lincoln Hall," *Alumni Quarterly,* 6:1 (Jan. 1912), 1.

3. White to American Terra Cotta Company, Mar. 20, 1911, 708, Terra Cotta Panels; White to Saxe, Mar. 23, 1911, 708, Zimmerman.

4. White to James, Apr. 3, 1911, 2/5/3, 22.

5. Moss to Greene, Apr. 1, 1911, 15/1/5, 7.

6. James to Zimmerman, Apr. 12, 1911, 2/5/3, 22.

7. Gates to James, Apr. 19, 1911, 2/5/3, 22, and see Greene to Saxe, Apr. 10, 1911, 15/1/5, 7; Saxe to Greene, Apr. 15, 1911, 15/1/5, 7.

8. Gates to James, Apr. 19, 1911, and see Gates to Zimmerman, Apr. 19, 1911, both in 2/5/3, 22.

9. Board of Trustees, *26th Report,* Apr. 27, 1911, 113; James to Gates, Apr. 26, 1911, and see James to Zimmerman, Apr. 26, 1911, 2/5/3, 22; Greene to James, Apr. 21, 1911, 2/5/3, 22; Greene to Gates, Apr. 21, 1911, 15/1/5, 7.

10. Board of Trustees, *26th Report,* Apr. 27, 1911, 113; Gates to James, Apr. 28, 1911, 2/5/3, 22.

Lincoln Quotations

1. Anthony J. Janata (Assistant to Kinley), Feb. 27, 1928; Pease to Janata, Mar. 3, 1928; Kinley to Pease, Mar. 6, 1928, all in Theodore C. Pease Papers, University Archives, 15/13/23; White to Kinley, June 8, 1928, and see White's list of "Inscriptions for Lincoln Hall Addition," Apr. 26, 1929, both in 709, Terra Cotta. See also Greene to

Zimmerman, May 25, 1910, 2/5/3, 22; list of Lincoln writings with Nicolay and Hay citations, in Greene's hand, 15/1/5, 10.

2. Greene to White, May 2, 1911, 708, Greene; Clerk of the Works [H. D. Oberdorfer] to English Brothers, May 3, 5, 31, 1911, all in 708, General Contract file; and see Oberdorfer to Greene, Aug. 19, 1912, and Greene's endorsement, Sept. 2, 1912, 708, Greene.

3. *The Collected Works of Abraham Lincoln,* edited by Roy P. Basler; Marion Delores Pratt and Lloyd A. Dunlap, assistant editors. 9 vols. New Brunswick, N.J.: Rutgers University Press, 1953–55.

4. Brown, who lived in Island Grove, Illinois, west of Springfield, had been a state legislator for several terms.

5. Lincoln's letter, written for his friend Conkling to read at a Union rally in Springfield, defended the Emancipation Proclamation.

6. Addressing a group led by Corning, a New York entrepreneur, Lincoln defended the need on occasion to suspend the writ of habeas corpus.

7. Gurney was a member of the Religious Society of Friends.

Portraits of Lincoln's Contemporaries

1. Greene, "The Meaning of Lincoln Hall," 1.

2. Greene to Zimmerman, Mar. 20, 1911, in which Greene referred to his list of published sources that he sent to Zimmerman, the list in turn being based on 3" × 5" notecards; Greene to Carriel, May 1, 1911; Carriel to Greene, n.d.; Greene to Carriel, May 6, 1911; Greene to Oglesby, May 2, 1911; and see Greene to American Terra Cotta and Ceramic Company, May 16, 1911, all 15/1/5, 7; and Greene to American Terra Cotta and Ceramic Company, June 15, 1911, 15/1/5, 10.

3. Greene to Zimmerman, Feb. 27, 1911; Gates to Zimmerman, Mar. 15, 1911; and see Greene to Zimmerman, Mar. 10, 20, 1911, 15/1/5, 7.

4. "The Original List of Names for the Six Escutcheons at the Corners of Lincoln Hall," enclosed with Greene to James, Sept. 26, 1910, 2/5/3, 22. In another copy of this list, evidently retyped from the one cited, Greene crossed out "Original" and wrote "Provisional," 15/1/5, 7.

5. James to Greene, Oct. 11, 1911, 15/1/5, 7; James, "Jonathan Baldwin Turner," *Alumni Quarterly,* 6:3 (July 1912), 188. Historians differ as to Turner's importance in the land-grant movement, just as they differ as to whether the University of Illinois, which traces itself to the Land-Grant Act Lincoln signed, should assume the moniker "Mr. Lincoln's University." See Winton U. Solberg, *The University of Illinois, 1867–1894: An Intellectual and Cultural History* (Urbana: University of Illinois Press, 1968), 22–23 and 56–57.

6. "Original List of Names," enclosed with Greene to James, Sept. 26, 1910, 2/5/3, 22.

7. "Original List;" Greene to Zimmerman, Feb. 20, 1911, both in 2/5/3, 22.

8. James to Greene, Oct. 11, 1910, 15/1/5, 7; Scott to Greene, Oct. 11, 1910, 2/5/3, 22; Greene to James, Oct. 12, 1910, 2/5/3, 22; *Recollected Words of Abraham Lincoln,* comp. and ed. Don E. Fehrenbacher and Virginia Fehrenbacher (Stanford, Calif.: Stanford University Press, 1996), 324, 326; Ida M. Tarbell, *The Life of Abraham Lincoln* (New York: Lincoln History Society, 1902), 3:148–49.

9. Weber to Greene, Oct. 10, 1910; Schmidt to Greene, Oct. 8, 1910; Rammelkamp to Greene, Oct. 7, 1910; Selby to Greene, Oct. 8, 1910; J. A. James to Greene, n.d.; Carr to Greene, note on Greene to Carr, Sept. 26, 1910; Cunningham to Greene, Sept. 28, 1910; and notes, all in 15/1/5, 7.

10. James to Greene, Oct. 11, 1910, 15/1/5, 7.

11. Greene to Zimmerman, Feb. 20, 1911, 15/1/5, 7; White to Zimmerman, Feb. 20, 1911, 708, Zimmerman; Saxe to Greene, Mar. 13, 1911, 15/1/5, 7.

Other Exterior Details

1. See James to Greene, Oct. 18, 1910, 2/5/3, 22; Greene to American Terra Cotta and Ceramic Company, May 2, 1911, 15/1/5, 7.
2. Pease to White, May 25, 1929, David Kinley Papers, University Archives, 2/6/1, 188, and see White to Kinley, May 27, 1929, ibid.; White to Pease, June 17, 1929, including Pease's note on the back listing Fessenden, Johnson, and Hamlin, Pease Papers, 15/13/23.
3. Owls, at once mythological and whimsical, were not uncommon as ornamentation in the period. For example, in Urbana, three owls still preside over the main entrance of the high school, which Joseph Royer designed in 1914. For Schneider's versatility in modeling owls and other creatures, see several issues of *Common Clay* as reprinted in Berry, *American Terra Cotta*, 120, 128, 133–35, 141, 145, 151, 175, 268.

Lincoln Hall's Memorial Hall

1. James M. White, "Lincoln Hall," *Alumni Quarterly*, 4:2 (Apr. 1910), 106; Greene to James, Nov. 10, 1909; Zimmerman to James, Nov. 13, 1909, 2/5/3, 22.
2. Greene to James, Feb. 21, 1911, 2/5/3, 22; Greene to Dodge, Feb. 27, 1911, 15/1/5, 7.
3. Greene to Zimmerman, Feb. 27, 1911; White to Greene, Feb. 28, 1911; Green to Zimmerman, Mar. 17, 1911, all in

15/1/5, 7; Greene to Zimmerman, July 12, 1911, 2/5/3, 22; Zimmerman to White, June 20, 30, 1911, 708, Zimmerman; James to Greene, July 13, 1911, 15/1/5, 10; James to White, July 13, 1911, 2/5/6, 18; White to Zimmerman, July 5, 1911, 708, Zimmerman; White to F. P. Smith, Oct. 31, 1911, repeating Greene's attached note, 708, Tablet Speech.
4. Spierling & Linden to Zimmerman, Aug. 30, 1911, 708, Zimmerman.

The Dedication of Lincoln Hall

1. "Tentative Program, Lincoln Hall Dedication, October 26–28," [1911], 2/5/3, 22; Greene to James, June 20, July 3, 1911, 2/5/3, 22; Greene to James, Aug. 17, 1911, and related note, n.d., 15/1/5, 10. (Nicolay had died in 1901.)
2. James to Greene, Aug. 7, 1911, 15/1/5, 10; Lincoln to James, July 16, 1911, 2/5/3, 22.
3. James to Taft, Aug. 9, 1911; James to Mann, Aug. 15, 1911; McKinley to James, Aug. 17, 1911; James to Charles D. Hilles (Secretary to the President), Aug. 17, 1911; Hilles to Deneen, Aug. 14, 1911; Cullom to James, Aug. 23, 1911, all in 2/5/3, 22.
4. Greene to James, June 20, 1911; James to Wilson, Aug. 14, 1911; Wilson to James, Aug. 17, 1911, all in 2/5/3, 22.
5. Greene to A. Ross Hill (and similar letters to others on the program), Sept. 6, 1911, 15/1/5, 10; Greene to American Terra Cotta and Ceramics Company, May 15, 1911, 15/1/5, 7, and June 15, 20, 1911; Gates to Zimmerman, July 13, 1911; Gates to English Bros., Sept. 8, 1911, all in 15/1/5, 10.
6. White to Greene, Aug. 19, 1912, and Greene's attached note, Sept. 2, 1912, 708, Greene.
7. Arthur H. Daniels to Hill, Jan. 29, 1913, 15/1/5, 12; program, *Dedication of Lincoln Hall, University of Illinois* (Urbana?:

University of Illinois, 1913); Dunne, "On the Dedication of Lincoln Hall," in *Dunne: Judge, Mayor, Governor,* comp. and ed. William L. Sullivan (Chicago: Windermere Press, 1916), 411.

8. Daniels to Joseph Manley, Jan. 25, 1913; Lewis to James, Jan. 2, 1913; Daniels to Lewis, Jan. 18, 1913, all in 15/1/5, 12.

9. James to Lincoln, Oct. 22, 1912, 2/5/3, 34; James to Daniels, Dec. 12, 1912, 15/1/5, 12; Fell papers, Illinois History and Lincoln Collections, University of Illinois Library.

10. James, "Draft of a letter to the editor of newspapers in re Lincoln Hall Dedication," Nov. 1, 1912, 2/5/3, 34; Daniels to James, Jan. 6, Mar. 12, 1913, both in 15/1/5, 12; James to Members of the Faculty, Feb. 10, 1913; James to Henry Wade Rogers, Feb. 20, 1913, both in 2/5/3, 34. In his second letter to James, Daniels enclosed two lists, one listing institutions that sent greetings "in response to the invitation to attend" the dedication, and the other listing "delegates of various colleges and universities" who did attend, newspapers and journals that were represented, and other guests.

11. [Evarts B. Greene], *Lincoln Hall, University of Illinois,* 8 pages, and *Lincoln Hall, University of Illinois: Dedicated to the Study of the Humanities,* 16 pages. The contract for the printing of these items by the Illinois Printing Company, Danville, Illinois, is dated Nov. 8, 1912, 2/5/3, 34.

12. Lincoln to John Maclean, Dec. 27, 1864, *Collected Works,* 8:184.

From the Centennial to the Bicentennial

1. White to P. and J. Corbett, Chicago, Sept. 27, 1912, 708, General Contract.

2. White to Taft, Mar. 13, 1923; Taft to White, Mar. 21, 1923, 708, Lincoln Bust.

3. White to Taft, Mar. 23, 1923; Taft to White, May 11, 1923; White to Kinley, May 15, 1923; White to Taft, May 19, 1923, all in 708, Lincoln Bust.

4. Inscription on the pedestal of Taft's statue, on a plaque now missing but quoted in F. Lauriston Bullard, *Lincoln in Marble and Bronze* (New Brunswick, N.J.: Rutgers University Press, 1952), 264; *Daily Illini,* June 19, 1925, 3:4.

5. William Sener Rusk, "The Rinehart Scholars" (entry for MacNeil), in Rusk, *William Henry Rinehart, Sculptor* (Baltimore, Md.: Norman T. A. Munder, 1939), 89–91; [Jessie Palmer Weber], "Awards Lincoln Statue Prizes" [Table of Contents title: "Lincoln and Douglas Statues: The Competition"], *Journal of the Illinois State Historical Society,* 7:3 (Oct. 1914), 300–301; [Ruckstull], "Lincoln the Lawyer," *Art World,* 3:5 (Feb. 1918), 366–68. See also "Speech at Petersburg, Illinois," Aug. 30, 1856, *Collected Works,* 2:366–68.

6. Lorado Taft, *Modern Tendencies in Sculpture* (Chicago: University of Chicago Press, 1921), 131–32 and fig. 383; W. W. Wiseman (Grand Central Art Galleries) to White, Oct. 12, 1928, Muriel Scheinman Papers, University Archives, 26/20/131; White to Kinley, Nov. 12, 1928, annotated by Kinley, 2/6/1, 188; Board of Trustees, *35th Report,* Nov. 16, 1928, 78. See also Donald Charles Durman, *He Belongs to the Ages: The Statues of Abraham Lincoln* (Ann Arbor: Edwards Brothers, 1951), 143–45, and Muriel Scheinman, *A Guide to Art at the University of Illinois: Urbana-Champaign, Robert Allerton Park, and Chicago* (Urbana: University of Illinois Press, 1995), 42–43.

7. Letter of Allan B. Rayburn (Student's Union), referred to White (White's reply was then referred to the Trustees), Council of Administration minutes, 10:179 (Dec. 2, 1913) and 10:191 (Dec. 19, 1913), University Archives; Board of Trustees, *31st Report,* June 13, 1921, July 6, 1921, 235–36, 8; White to Kinley, June 25, 1921, 708, Miscellaneous.

8. *Daily Illini,* Feb. 17, 1923, 6:3; July 29, 1921, 2:3; Jan. 9, 1935, 2:3–4; Jan. 12, 1935, 2:3.

9. *Daily Illini,* Oct. 4, 1925, 2:4; Oct. 29, 1926, 12:2; Feb. 13, 1929, 1:4; Nov. 11, 1930, 4:3; Sept. 24, 1931, 4:1; Feb. 15, 1929, 4:2; Jan. 12, 1935, 2:3.

10. White to Board of Trustees, June 7, 1926, in Board of Trustees, *34th Report,* July 7, 1926, 86, and Aug. 19, 1927, 424.

11. Board of Trustees, *34th Report,* Oct. 12, 1927, 477; May 23, 1928, 616–17.

12. White to Kinley, Jan. 16, 1928, 2/6/1, 188.

13. Board of Trustees, July 17, 1929, *35th Report,* 262–63. See also "A Brief History of Lincoln Hall," unsigned paper (1991), 8, 10–11, in Lincoln Hall folder, University Archives; and White to Louis A. Warren, Oct. 28, 1930, 26/20/131.

14. George A. Berry III, with Sharon S. Darling, *Bars and Blades: A History of TC Industries, 1881–2006* (Crystal Lake, Ill.: TCR Corp., 2008), 30.

15. "Life of Lincoln," *Clay-Worker,* 608.

16. Conversation with the author, May 15, 2008.

17. [Greene], *Lincoln Hall,* 4.

PHOTO CREDITS

Abraham Lincoln Presidential Library and Museum (courtesy Mary Michals and Roberta Fairburn), 10.

Butler University, University Archives, Donald Charles Durman Collection (courtesy Sally Childs-Helton), 94 (left).

Common Clay, 1:4 (Oct. 1920), 18 (right), 19 (top).

Sharon S. Darling, 18 (left).

Thomas A. Freeburg (by arrangement with Linda Corteen, Husmann Elementary School, Crystal Lake, Ill.), 44-47.

Handbook of Architects and Builders, ed. Charles R. Adams (Chicago, Wm. Johnson Printing Co., 1900), 6 (bottom).

Nick Mann: ii, iv–v, vi, vii, 3, 70, 76 (bottom), 79, 82-83, 85, 94 (right), 95, 97, 100

Planning Division, Facilities and Services, University of Illinois at Urbana-Champaign: Melvyn Skvarla, 17, 19 (bottom pair); J. Todd Hearn, 20-21; Seth Gunnerson, 73, 89, 99, 101, 102 (both).

University Archives, University of Illinois at Urbana-Champaign: (image number in parenthesis), x (1618), 4 (3791), 6 (top, 3739), 7 (1878), 8 (right, 3736), 9 (2257), 14 (1879), 15 (3792), 51 (3741), 75 (3790), 78 (3742), 90 (3737), 91 (3738), 98 (3744), 103 (1881); also ix, 5, 8 (in 37/2/11).

David B. Wiegers: i, 12-13, 16, 22-43, 48-49, 52-53, 55-58, 60-65, 69, 71, 74, 76 (top left and right), 77, 80-81, 88, 90-91, 96, 99, 101, 105.

INDEX

JOHN HOFFMANN was raised in Springfield, Illinois.
He is presently the curator of the Illinois History and
Lincoln Collections of the University of Illinois Library
at Urbana-Champaign. He has written widely on
Lincoln, the Civil War, and Illinois history.

The University of Illinois Press
is a founding member of the
Association of American University Presses.

Composed in 12/16 Adobe Garamond Pro
by Erin Kirk New
for the University of Illinois Press
Designed by Erin Kirk New
Manufactured by Four Colour Imports, Ltd.

University of Illinois Press
1325 South Oak Street
Champaign, IL 61820-6903
www.press.uillinois.edu